Cordialement
Charles E Stubbs 9/25/78

D0983316

BEIHEFTE ZUR
ZEITSCHRIFT FÜR ROMANISCHE PHILOLOGIE

BEGRÜNDET VON GUSTAV GRÖBER
FORTGEFÜHRT VON WALTHER VON WARTBURG
HERAUSGEGEBEN VON KURT BALDINGER

Band 145

CHARLES E. STEBBINS

A Critical Edition of the
13th and 14th Centuries
Old French Poem Versions
of the ›Vie de Saint Alexis‹

MAX NIEMEYER VERLAG TÜBINGEN
1974

To
Jan A. Nelson
my teacher, my colleague and my friend

ISBN 3-484-52049-3

© Max Niemeyer Verlag Tübingen 1974
Alle Recht vorbehalten. Printed in Germany
Satz: ewe Klingeis Böblingen
Einband von Heinr. Koch Tübingen

TABLE OF CONTENTS

But the state of the Saints is warm and bright: for they live and walk
in the noon-tide and see with open and enlightened eyes the brightness
of the Sun, for the glory of God flows through them . . . Their bare
understanding is drenched through by the Eternal Brightness even as the
air is drenched through by sunshine.

Ruysbroeck

I. A CRITICAL EDITION OF THE THIRTEENTH
   CENTURY OLD FRENCH POEM VERSION OF THE
   VIE DE SAINT ALEXIS

INTRODUCTION

The present edition of this Old French version of the *Vie de Saint Alexis* will fill a lacuna of long standing in Alexis studies. The text, composed in the Picard dialect in the thirteenth century, is preserved in two manuscripts: *P*, located in Paris at the Bibl. nat., fr. 2162; *O*, found in Oxford, Bodl., Canonici misc. 74[1]. Despite the interest, both historical and literary, of this version of the Alexis legend, no truly critical edition of its text has thus far been undertaken. This then is the aim of the present study[2].

The selection of *P* as the base MS. of the present edition is an obvious choice. It is highly unlikely that the scribes of either *O* or *P* had recourse to the

---

1 My complete edition of the Oxford MS. (*O*) has appeared in *Romania*, tome 92 (1971), pp. 1-36.

There is also a poem in octosyllabic rhymed couplets belonging to the early 13th century which is preserved in a manuscript copy (*R*) located in the Bibl. nat., fr. 25408, fol. 36.

2 P served as the base MS. of the present edition with variants from O. Joseph Herz, *De Saint Alexis, eine afrz. Alexiuslegende aus dem 13. Jrh.* Frankfort, 1879, published the only other edition of this 13th century version. He proceeded, however, in an eclectic manner in establishing the text, using essentially P as the base MS., but also incorporating readings from O into the base MS. where they were called for by grammar or metrics, or where they corresponded more logically or at least seemed to correspond more logically to the thought. In addition, Herz, for the sake of orthographic uniformity, obliterated many of the most salient characteristics of the base MS. P, for example, shows the peculiarity that pre-consonantal l following vowels frequently disappears: *pamier, escoter, atre, saver, abe, mavais, amosne*, etc. (See Phonology, L). Herz invariably uses the forms with u after declaring that this characteristic of the base MS. (i.e., the loss of the l) is "worthy of attention." Moreover, in order to identify the "hard" pronunciation of g before e, Herz writes gu throughout. The MS., however, consistently offers only g which is characteristic of the Picard dialect (See Phonology, G, a) and therefore should have been preserved, especially after Herz himself declared that the dialect of the poem was Picard. Several puzzling changes of the same nature could be cited.

G. Koerting, *ZrP*, IV (1880), 175-78, judged Herz's edition rather harshly. He questions the validity of such a "hybrid" or "hypothetical" text and considers such text reconstructions as rather dangerous experiments which possess only "problematic value." His concluding remarks (pp. 176-177) in which he favors a more truly critical edition greatly influenced my decision to re-edit the text: „Nach unserer Ansicht hätte der Herausgeber, statt durch Combination einen neuen Text herzustellen, besser

Latin Model. Hence, the greater originality and creativity found in P with respect to the Latin source[3] is to be attributed to the author of the lost original copy (X)[4]. The fact that P shows a better treatment of the material indicates that the scribe or his predecessors in that line of descent from X innovated the least, and that the changes or deformations occurred in the collateral branch (X^1). P best preserves the state of X and thus is a more genuine copy of the original than is O. O, on the other hand, exhibits a marked tendency toward the abbreviation of certain passages which at times disturbs the continuity of the poem. Moreover, the scribe of O carelessly omitted the nasal stroke in a considerable number of words: *sait* for sai[n]t, *quat* for qua[n]t, *pardeir* for pard[on]eir, etc. Some of these words have remained indecipherable resulting in a number of obscure and, at times, unintelligible hemistiches.

In establishing the text, I have remained faithful to the orthography and morphology of the base MS. Sporadic emendations have been made only to render a verse intelligible and all additions placed in brackets are either obvious emendations or taken from the variant MS. The second table at the foot of the page contains rejected readings from the base MS.

Modern punctuation and capitalization have been introduced, and I have followed in general the recommendations of the committee of the *Société des anciens textes français*[5] in the use of accents, diareses, distinction of the vocalic and the consonantal i and j, u and v, numbering of lines, and indication of the beginning of the columns of each folio of the base MS. All abbreviations have been solved in accordance with those instances where the same words occur in their full form. Roman numerals have also been uniformly transcribed in letter form.

---

gethan, die Texte von O und P in ihrer ursprunglichen Gestalt neben einander abdrukken zu lassen, unter Berichtigung natürlich der offenbaren Fehler, wobei aber die Lesarten der Handschriften unter dem Text hätten angegeben werden müssen. Man würde dann wenigstens ein deutliches Bild von der Gestaltung einer jeden der beiden Redactionen erhalten haben . . . Eine andere Möglichkeit wäre gewesen, den Text von P allein zu geben und die Varianten von O in den Noten aufzuführen. Sicher hätte ein derartiges Verfahren eine bessere Uebersicht über den Stand der handschriftlichen Tradition geboten, als es bei dem von dem Herausgeber beliebten geschehen ist."

3 The source of our 13th century Old French poem is the Latin prose legend entitled "Vita S. Alexii Confessoris" and published in the *Acta Sanctorum Bollandiorum*, Tome IV, month of July, 251-253. See my article "Relationship of the Paris MS. 2162 (Bibl. nat.) to its Latin Source" which follows this critical edition.

4 We are inclined to accept the following relationship between the two MSS:

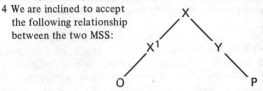

5 See *Romania* 52 (1926), pp. 244-49.

1. Versification of *P*

The text of *P* contains 1224 verses divided into 60 monorhymed Alexandrine laisses, 49 masculine and 11 feminine, with 17 different masculine assonances and 6 different feminine assonances. The cesura is regularly after the sixth syllable and our text rarely errs in the matter of syllable-count. The deviations from the various rhyme schemes are given in parentheses as they occur in the MS.

Masculine Laisses

ain,	laisse XLIV.
	Plain 895 (PLENUM) is the only word in which -*ain* (derived from tonic close *e* + nasal) assonates with -*ain* (derived from tonic *a* + nasal); see Phonology, Vowels. E (close), c.
ait,	laisse XXV.
ant,	laisse LII
é, ét,	laisses III (but *roés* 32, *engoulés* 33, *refusés* 68), XIII (but *entrés* 330, *pensés* 341, *encombrés* 351), XVI (but *amer* 405, *eürés* 423), XVII, XLII (but *parler* 857, *envolepés* 861), LV (but *ralumés* 1107), LIX.
ent,	laisses VIII, XL, XLIII, LVII.
	Garant 214 is the only word in which -*ant* assonates with -*ent*. See Phonology, Vowels. E (close), footnote 2.
er,	laisses VI (but *loier* 142, *entrafier* 146), X, XI, XXIV, XXVII, XXIX, XXXVIII, XLI, LVI.
és,	laisses IX (but *afiés* 277), XXX (but *oubliés* 660).
i, it,	laisses XIX (but *David* 455), XXI.
	For the retention of the final dental (loose), see Phonology, Dentals, c.
ier,	laisses VII, XV, XX (but *abaisiés* 467), XXVIII, XXXVII, LVIII.
iers,	laisse XXXI.
iés,	laisse XXXV.
in,	laisses XXII, XXXIII.
ir,	laisses IV, LI (but *nourit* 1027, *laidier* 1028, *fil* 1041).
is,	laisses XIV, XXVI (but *Alexins* 567, *peril* 570, *esclarcist* 576), XLV (but *paradys* 911).
or,	laisses V, XXXVI, XXXIX, LIV, LX (but *doçour* 1223, *signour* 1224).
ort,	laisse XLVII.
us,	laisse XII.

anche, ance,	laisse XLVIII.
ee,	laisses XVIII (but *dure* 440, *clame* 443), XXIII, XXXIV, XLIX, LIII.
ente,	laisse L (but *vestemenche* 1020).
este	laisse I.
ie,	laisses II, XLVI (but *martire* 923).
ure,	laisse XXXII (but *rancune* 693 and 694).

2. Language of P

The notes on phonology and morphology are intended primarily to assist the reader with some of the difficulties and anomalies of the manuscript forms. Like most manuscripts, *P* shows a mixture of dialect features attesting that the original or authorial copy has come down to us through an unknown series of intermediaries. However, sufficient diagnostic characteristics occur in *P* to safely maintain that our base manuscript originates from the 13th century and belongs to the Picard dialect.

In setting forth the characteristic features of the language of *P*, I shall start from the Vulgar Latin rather than from the Old French sounds.

3. Phonology

Vowels

A Pretonic *a* + palatal *l* > *i*: *travillier* 765 (VL* TRIPALIARE > *travaillier* > *trave (i) llier* > *travillier*); *travilier* 388, 475; *travilié* 1100; *traviliés* 727. The development of pretonic *a* + palatal *l* > *i* is an analogous formation with that of pretonic *e* (close and open) + palatal *l, n* > Picard *i/ei/e*. The forms in *ei/e*, which are Francien, are frequently found in Old Picard texts together with those in *i*[1].

E (close). (a) Tonic free close *e* invariably diphthongizes to *oi*[2]. No vestiges of the earlier *ei* diphthong are recorded.

(b) The forms *iaus* 43 and 786 are Picard. The phonetic development of VL - ELLOS (CL - ILLOS) > *iaus, eaus, aus,* distinguishes Old Picard from the Francien *eus*[3].

(c) Tonic close *e* before a nasal may be spelled *ain: maine* 927, 971, 1063

---

1 See Charles Théodore Gossen, *Petite grammaire de l'ancien picard* (Paris, 1951), # 34.
2 *Oi* is characteristic of Picard. See Gossen, # 16.
3 Gossen, # 12b.

(VL MINAT); *plain* 230, 895, 1160 (PLENUM); etc. This trait distinguishes the Old Picard dialect from all neighboring dialects. Old Francien and the central Norman dialects have *ein*, while those of Burgundy and Lorraine, as well as Walloon, have *oin*, undoubtedly a posterior nasalization[4].

Rather frequently $\tilde{e} > \tilde{a}$[5], a feature usually ascribed to the Francien dialect[6]: *dolent* 411, 811, 916, etc. (VL* DOLENTUM); but *dolant* 373, 423, 427; *sens* 491; but *sans* 379, 525, 1003, etc.; *tens* 265, 358; but *tans* 15, 21, 94; etc.

(d) Pretonic close *e* + palatal *l* > Picard *i*: *vilier* 66, 360, 717, etc. (VIGILARE); *mervillier* 623 (VL* MERIBILIARE); *consillier* 189, *aparillier* 790, 798, 1166 (VL* APPARICULARE); *esmervilier* 652; etc.; but *veliés* 726 (VIGILATIS); and *consellier* 468 (CONSILIARIUM). See pretonic *a* + palatal *l*. Cf. pretonic open *e* + palatal *l, n.*

The tonic vowel, however, is apparently strong enough to resist umlauting. Tonic close *e* + palatal *l* occurs as *e: consel* 38, 572, 870 (CONSILIUM); *mervelle* 764, 774, 902, etc. (VL* MERIBILIAM). Cf. tonic open *e* + palatal *l.*

E (open). (a) Tonic open *e* + *wau* > *ieu/eu*[7], with the former predominating: *Dieu* 4, 58, 81, 98, etc. (DEUM); *Diex* 45, 52, 131, etc. (DEUS); but *Deu* 19, 35, 40, etc.; and *Dex* 56, 243.

Note *Dé* (DEUM) 107. *Dé* is generally used in exclamatory expressions. Cf. *en non Dé, pour l'amour Dé, de par Dé,* etc. (See Gossen, # 9, e).

(b) The forms *-iau/-el/-iel* (-ELLUS) are Picard[8]: *biax* 397, 467, 932, etc. (x=us); but *biel* 135, 448, etc.; *bel* 876; etc.

(c) Pretonic open *e* + palatal *l* > Picard *i*: *millor* 116, 468 (MELIOREM); *milors* 376. See pretonic *a* + palatal *l*. Cf. pretonic close *e* + palatal *l.* However, tonic open *e* + palatal *l* diphthongizes regularly: *vielart* 296, 557; *viellart* 712; *vielle* 53; etc. Cf. tonic close *e* + palatal *l.*

(d) Pretonic open *e* + palatal *n* > *i/e,* with the former predominating: *signor* 383, 737, 823, 1213, etc. (SENIOREM); *signour* 1224, but *segnor* 415, 644; and *segnorie* 10, 27. See pretonic *a* + palatal *l*. Cf. pretonic *e* (close and open) + palatal *l.*

I (close). Tonic or pretonic close *i* exhibits normal phonetic development.

O (close). (a) Initial unaccented close *o* (free or checked) > *ou/o* [u]: *douter* 542 (DUBITARE); but *doter* 639; *souspirer* 537, 773 (SUSPIRARE); but

---

4 Gossen, # 19. Cf. Kr. Nyrop, *Grammaire historique de la langue française* (Gyldendal, 1967), # 216.

5 *En* and *an* are identical in sound as attested by the rhyme *entent: garant* 213:214.

6 Nyrop, # 215. Cf. Gossen, # 15.

7 For the treatment of tonic open *e* + *wau* > *ieu/eu,* see E. Schwan and D. Behrens, *Grammaire de l'ancien français,* trad. O. Bloch (Leipzig, 1923), # 20, 1, and # 51, 1. Cf. Gossen, # 9.

8 Gossen, # 12a.

sospire 623, 810, 814 (SUPIRAT); *souffrir* 934, 1012; *soufrir* 89, 1030
(VL* SUFFERIRE); but *sofrir* 1025; etc.

(b) Tonic free close *o* > *o/ou,* with *ou* frequently > *eu: amor* 1191, 1200
(AMOREM); *douchor* 123 (Low Latin DULCOREM); *dolor* 434, 565, 952,
etc. (DOLOREM); etc.; but *doçour* 1223; *signour* 1224 (SENIOREM);
dolouse 430 (VL* DOLOSAT); etc.; and *espeuse* 23, 39, 819, etc. (SPO
[N] SAM); *seul* 625, 1087, etc. (SOLUM); etc.

O (open). Tonic free open *o* > *ue,* which frequently > *eu: puet* 312, 536, 598,
etc. (VL* POTET); *cuer* 211, 356, 899, etc. (COR); *nuef* 410 (NOVUM);
trueve 501 (VL* TROPAT); *truevent* 751; etc.; but *treuve* 205; *peule* 166,
721, 730, etc. (POPULUM); *euvre* 2, 16, 750, etc. (OPERAM); etc.

U (close). Tonic or pretonic close *u* invariably occurs as *u: jurer* 644
(JURARE); *dure* 932, 979, 1015 (DURAM); *huchier* 192, 466 (VL* HUC-
CARE); etc.

Consonants

C (a) Initial *c* + *a* > *c* [k], with only sporadic variations: *cambre* 168, 171,
176, etc.; *cangier* 390; *cartre* 715, 844, 896; *ciere* 268; *cief* 475, 544, etc.;
but *chartre* 892; *chiés* 216; *chiere* 854; etc.
The use of *c* is characteristic of Picard [9].

(b) The significant orthographic variation that occurs in our text for [ts] is
between *c/ss* (standard OF) and *ch* (characteristic of Northern French).
The spelling *ch* which, in the 14th century, triumphs in the entire Picard
domain [10] abounds: *commenche* 539, 548, 631, etc.; *trache* 343; *penitanche*
685; *fache* 772, 816; and practically the entire rhyming scheme of Laisse
XLVIII.

G (a) In the Picard dialect, *g* + *a* (der. from Latin words) and *g* + *a, e, i* (der.
from Germanic words), whether initial or supported (see *longe,* etc., below) >
[g], which may be spelled *g, gh, gu,* with the form *g* predominating [11].
Our text consistently employs the *g* form with only sporadic deviations:
garder 106, 144, 265, etc.; *garir* 198, 1050; *garnie* 15, 317; *gerpir* 105;
gerpi 488, 1203; *longe* 1006; *longement* 817; but *guie* 20, 875; *guise* 473,
605.
The literary character of *joïr* 1047 (VL* GAUDIRE), and *joie* 72, 138, 858
(GAUDIAM) explains the frequency of the Francien Form [12].
The form *aigue* 676, 837 (VL ACQUAM) is borrowed from the regions of
Lyonnais and Dauphiné [13]. The development of CL AQUA is complex and
abounds in dialectal variants. The form *aigue* (Cf. Old Provencal *aigua/aiga*)

9 Gossen, # 41.   12 Gossen, # 42a.
10 Gossen, # 38.   13 Gossen, # 43.
11 Gossen, # 42.

may be derived from the widely attested VL form ACQUA(AKWA) in the following way: AKWA > aiwa; a phonetic *g* develops between *ai* and *wa*: hence *aigwa*, then *aigue* by definitive elimination of *w*[14].

(b) Intervocalic *g* shows regular phonetic development. Note, however, the maintenance of *g* in the following learned words: (1) preceding tonic *u* or *o*: *agus* 326 (ACUTOS) and *vigor* 115[15]; (2) preceding atonic *u*: *segurtain* 894 (=OF *segurain* < VL* SECURANUM) and *aseguranche* 960 (on VL* ASSECURARE)[16].

(c) In paroxytones the *g* is sometimes assimilated by a final close *o* < *u* which then develops as *wau* with the tonic vowel[17]: *feu* 564 (FOCUM) and *peu* 121 (PAUCUM); but *poi* in verses 927, 1040, 1061, etc., where the final *g* has undoubtedly gone to *yod*[18]. (Cf. *pai* < PACO.)

L In the combination *a* + *l* + consonant, *l* either becomes vocalized or is lost with vocalization predominating: *esbaudir* 92; *eshaucier* 182; *paumier* 635, 1021; *fauser* 158; *autre* 56, 182, 393, etc.; etc.; but *pamier* 605, 679 (PALMARIUM); *atre* 1084; *saver* 243, 288, 540, etc. (SALVARE); *saveté* 348; *abe* 744, 842 (VL ALBAM); *mavais* 269, 479; *savage* 972; invariably *amosne* 393, 407, 615, etc. (VL* ALEMOSINAM); *amosnier* 172 (VL* ALEMOSINARIUM); *hate* 1060; but *haut* elsewhere; etc.

In Old Picard, the normal development is the vocalization of the *l*, the loss of the *l* being exceptional. The forms *saver, savage, mavais* (having no equivalent forms in Modern Picard) are probably borrowed from Walloon. The forms *pamier* and *amosne*, however, have subsisted in Modern Picard as *pamier* and *amone*[19].

Note 1: We invariably find either *al* or *a* (=*a le*), never *au*: *al* 13, 74, etc.; *a* 78, etc.; and either *as* or *a* (=*a les*), never *aus*: *as* 110, etc.; *a* 403, etc.

Note 2: The spelling *x* (=*us*) further attests the fact that *l* generally vocalizes to *u* in our text. See *X*.

Note 3: Sporadically the *l* is retained: *malmis* 569, 918.

M (a) Except for *hom* 28, 338, 399 (HOMO), final *m* has consistently been reduced to *n*: *on* 30, 73, 559, etc. (HOMO); *non* 336, 519, 900 (NOMEN); *fain* (FAMEN); *mon* 209, etc.; *son* 8, etc.; etc.[20]

---

14 See J. Anglade, *Grammaire de l'ancien provençal* (Paris, 1921), p. 171 Rem. Cf. Gustav Körting, *Lateinisch-Romanisches Wörterbuch* (New York, 1923), # 780 and M. K. Pope, *From Latin To Modern French with especial consideration of Anglo-Norman* (Manchester-England, 1952), # 330.

15 For the development of *agus* and *vigor*, see O. Bloch et W. v. Wartburg, *Dictionnaire étymologique de la langue française* (Paris, 1964), pp. 14 and 673.

16 See Körting, # 8560 and # 955. 18 Nyrop, # 417, 1.

17 Nyrop, # 201 Rem. and # 248. 19 Gossen, # 58.

20 Our scribe was very consistent in his orthography of the final nasal consonant. *Hom* is invariably found as *hom*, never as *hon*, except with the inflexional -s; *non* (NOMEN) is always spelled *non*, never *nom*; *en* (IN) is invariably found as *en*, never as *em*; etc. From the above examples, we may safely conclude that alternative orthographic forms rarely occur in this text.

(b) Final *m* in the oblique singular has been retained in some Latin proper names: *Sarram* 455; *Jhesum* 1193; but usually the final *m* has been lost: *Sarra* 47; *Jhesu* 332, 911.

N (a) *N* has been inserted in a number of words (perhaps by confusion of prefixes: *ex/in*: *enstragne* 717 (EXTRANEUM); *ensïent* 202, 885 (SCIEN-TEM)[21]; *Alenxis 189; enspeuse* 322, 463 (SPONSAM); etc.

(b) Frequently labial *m* > dental *n* when a labial consonant follows, even when the labial consonant is not etymological: *ensanble* 40, 247, 453; but *ensamble* 227, 802, 925, etc.; *sanble* 252; *ramenbre* 47; *ramenbrement* 241; but *ramembrast* 627; etc.

(c) By dissimilation the consonantal group *n'm* occurs as *rm* in *arme* 697, 745, 962 (ANIMAM)[22] and *m'n* has become *mr* in *Damredieu* 271, 425, 540, etc.; *Damrediex* 567[23].

Note that *m* has been partially denasalized to *p* in *dampnés* 263 (DAMNA-TUS). This partial denasalization sometimes occurs in the pronunciation of Latin and early learned loan-words such as *damner* and *damnedeu*[24]. Cf. Old Provencal *domna/dompna*.

(d) After *r*, final *n* is invariably lost: *jor* 678, 781, 867, etc.; *sejor* 740, 785; etc.

N (palatal). Palatalized *n* in medial position is generally spelled *gn*: *signor* 383, 1201, 1213; *dagna* 52; *compagnie* 934; *ensegnier* 165; *engignier* 195.

However, sporadic orthographical deviations occur: *sanier* 155 (SIGNARE); *linage* 130, 148 (VL* LINEATICUM); but *lignage* 144; and *prengne* 345; *[j]oingnons* 228 (JUNGIMUS).

Labials

Labials exhibit normal phonetic development and necessitate few remarks except for the following:

(a) Note the loss or retention of labials in the following words: *baptesme* 79 (semi-learned); but *batesme* 55; *escripture* 688 (semi-learned); *escripte* 714; and invariably *peule*: 166, 721, 730, 1097, etc. (POPULUM); *peules* 788, 1085, etc.

The form *peule* is Picard and analogous with the substantives in -ABULUM/ -ABULAM, > *aule* (Cf. TABULAM > *taule*, FABULAM > *faule*, etc.)[25].

(b) In the secondary consonant group *m'l*, the forms without the glide

---

21 Cf. *mien ensïent*, vv. 579 and 594, in Adam le Bossu, *Le Jeu de la Feuillée*, ed. by E. Langlois (Paris, 1966).

22 See Schwan-Behrens, # 183 Rem.

23 The development of DOMINUM DEUM > *damredieu* is learned and presents a richness of forms particularly remarkable: *damledieu, dambredeu, damnedieu*, etc. See Schwan-Behrens, # 182 Rem. Cf. Pope, # 643.

24 Pope, # 369.

25 Gossen, # 52.

10

consonant *b* are characteristic of Picard, Walloon and Lotharingian[26]: *humle* 886; *asanler* 1129, 1134. However, as Gossen points out (p. 97), the influence of the Francien orthography seems to have been particularly great for this consonant cluster: *ensamble* 227, 925, 986, etc.; *asambler* 148; etc. Cf. Dentals, (e).

R (a) Sporadic examples of metathesis of the *r*[27] are found in *avresier* 479 (ADVERSARIUM); *avrisiers* 675; *herbrigier* 481, 613 (on *herberge*, or VL* HERIBERGARE); *govrener* 937, 1000 (GUBERNARE); for the standard Central French forms *aversier, herbergier, governer.*

(b) *R* has been generated by the process of assimilation in *frestraus* 151 (obl. pl. of OF *frestel* < VL* FISTELLA; see Glossary).

(c) The loss of *r* occurs in *mos* 1004 (MORS) because *r* has assimilated to *s* (*rs* > *s*) and is a useless letter. And since our scribe writes *rs* as *s* (i. e. since he writes *s* for *s* or *rs*), he may also write *s* as *rs*: *tors* (pronounced *tos*) 1071, 1084 (VL* TOTTOS). The form *tors* is especially significant because if the spelling *mos* (pronounced *mos*) gives us our first clue that *r* + *s* ceased to be pronounced, *tors* for *tos* clinches the argument.

The loss of *r* also occurs in *toterele* 1079 (VL TURTURELLA).

S (a) Etymological *s* has generally been retained before consonants including *m* and *n*, but sporadically it has been dropped, indicating that this *s* was probably not pronounced by our scribe: *defaé* 417 (*des,* + *faé* < VL* FATAM); *depané* 410, 428; *depane* (pres. 3) 926 (on OF *despaner* < *des,* + *paner*); *depanee* 973; *fit* 176; but *fist* elsewhere; *trek'en* 683; but *treske* 1036; etc.

(b) A non-etymological *s* has been inserted in *asmosnier* 393 (VL* ALEM-OSINARIUM); *crisne* 429 (CRINEM); and the possesive adjective *ses* has been spelled *ces* twice in verse 799.

Note 1: In Picard (as in Francien), effacement (amuïssement) generally occurs with *s* (interior) before consonant. (See a, above.) Scribal use of parasitic *s* (See b, above) is, therefore, purely orthographic. See Gossen, # 50.

Dentals (T, D)

(a) Intervocalic *t* or *d* is generally lost except for a considerable number of learned and semi-learned words: *vie* 3, 8, 87, etc.; *aeure* 200, 395 (ADORAT); *oïr* 91, 111, 150, etc. (AUDIRE); *muer* 835 (MUTARE); etc.; but *creator* 125, 745, 1186, etc.; *paradys* 481, 684, 911, etc.; *humilité* 35, 359, 840, etc.; etc.

(b) Final *t* or *d*, if fixed (i. e. supported by a consonant or the product of assimilation), becomes *t*: *grant* 27, 39, 43, etc.

Sporadically we find the removal of the final dental: *main* 867 (=*maint*); *quier* 777 (=*quiert* < QUAERIT).

---

26 Gossen, # 61.
27 The type *-er* > *-re* is the most frequent in Old Picard. See Gossen, # 57.

(c) Final dental, if loose (i. e. unsupported by a consonant or the product of assimilation), is either retained as *t*, or is lost, with the latter predominating: *foi* 41, 82 (FIDEM); *mue* 59 (MUTAT); *né* 72 (NATUM); *done* 45, 490, 505 (DONAT); etc.; but *oït* 482 (AUDITUM); *contét* 26, 848 (COMPUTATUM); *demorét* 849 (VL* DEMORATUM); *sonét* 852 (SONATUM); etc.[28]. Final *t* is generally lost in the preterite tense: *pora* 102, 129; *garda* 109; etc.

Final dentals, if loose, had disappeared from the pronunciation even if they were retained in the orthography. The following rhymes bear this out: *vreté:contét* 847:848; *apelé:sonét* 851:852; and *gari:David* 454:455;

(d) Dentals in secondary combinations with *s* > s. This is another trait of the Picard dialect[29]. Examples abound: *assés* 11, 49, etc.; *tos* 21, 23, 86, etc.; *grans* 62, 98, etc.; *piés* 138; *fois* 280; etc.

(e) The glide consonant *d* does not usually develop in the combination *n'r*: *tenrement* 200, 814, 884; *tenror* 1086; *venrai* 943; *venra* 480; *engenré* 334; *engenreüre* 689; but *cendre* 914, 982. The forms without *d* are characteristic of Picard. See Labials, (b).

The development of *d* in the future and conditional tenses of *voloir* also does not occur: *vora* 596; *voront* 1152; *voroie* 963, 1003; *voroit* 636, 919.

(f) *T* is found as *d* in *cordine* 448 (LOW LATIN CORTINAM) and *d* as *t* in *ytrope* 1108 (HYDROPICUM).

W In the Picard dialect of the northeast (Walloon and Lotharingian also), -*w*- (a fricative bilabial velar which was probably weakly pronounced) may develop after *u* in hiatus, id est, after the groups *au, ou, eu, iu,* preceding a vowel. This -*w*- subsists in Modern Walloon[30]. The following examples are recorded in our text: *euwist* 73 (=*euist*, < HABUISSET); *awan* 308 (HOC ANNO); *siuwe* 528 (=*soie*, poss. adj.); *leuwiers* 684 (LOCARIUM); *Ewangile* 204, 285, 500 (ECCL. LATIN EVANGELIUM); *Ewangiles* 341.

X *X* frequently occurs in our text, especially as the common abbreviation for *us*[31]: *biax* 397, 425, 433, etc.; *bias* occurs only once in v. 251; *viex* 461, 689, 820; *iex* 594, 619, 813, etc. (OCULOS); *Diex* 7, etc.; but *ceus* 57, 144, 176, etc.; *iaus* 43, 786 (ILLOS); and *as* (=*als*) 37, 138, 1165, etc.

We also find: *exemple* 25, 1206 (learned word); and *Alexins* 211, 257, 277, etc.

Y *Y* employed in lieu of *i* occurs quite frequently: *ymage* 329, 331, 518, etc.; *Syre* 318, 326 (SYRIAM); but *Sire* 381; *ayés* 239; but *aiés* 612; *dÿables* 682;

---

28 In Picard and Walloon, final dental (loose) was maintained longer than in Francien where it disappeared in the first quarter of the 12th century. (See Schwan-Behrens, # 274 Rem.)

29 Gossen, # 40.

30 Gossen, # 54.

31 Pope, # 733.

ydrope 1122 (HYDROPICUM); *ydrope* 1108; *castoyer* 1044 (CASTIGARE);
Z *Z* is found only once: *Zacharie* 53.

4. Morphology

The Definite Article
(a) The Picard form (Walloon also) *le* for Francien *la* in the oblique case of the feminine article [1] occurs sporadically in our text: *le haute deïté* 75; *le maison* 166; *le splendor* 871; *le joie* 1082; *le chartre* 892.
(b) Enclisis of the definite article in the masculine singular is invariably found after *en*: *el ciel* 6; *el lit* 186; *el mostier* 518; etc. Except for *du peule* 166 and *dou* 962, we consistently find *del*: *del fil* 50; *del siecle* 4, 35; etc.
In the plural of both genders, we invariably find *es* and *des*: *es mains* 745, 1197; *es voiles* 587; *des dois* 164; *des letres* 91, 92, 205; etc. Cf. enclitic forms of the personal pronoun, note 1.
(c) In the masculine nominative singular, elision may or may not occur: *l'apostoiles* 873, 894, 1088; *l'emperere* 883; but *li apostoiles* 1119, 1156; *li escris* 29, 337, *li enfes* 81, 89, 94, etc.

Substantive and Adjective. In general, the two case inflectional system is rigorously maintained [2]. The use of analogical -*s* confirms this. This is especially true in regard to the various rhyme schemes which religiously observe the distinction [3].
A superficial examination of the text, however, suffices to reveal the tendency to substitute the accusative for nominative in a limited number of words: *saint* 84, 196, 277, 364, etc.; *grant* 514; *tel* 912, 1069; etc.
The most salient characteristic found in our text is perhaps the presence of a non etymological inflectional -*s* in the nominative singular of masculine nouns originally of the classical third declension. Except for *pere* 203 [4], we invariably find *peres* 28, 72, 90, etc.; in the vocative singular *peres* appears in verses 397, 398; in the oblique case invariably *pere* 104, 170, 207, etc.
This inflectional -*s* in the nominative and vocative cases comes from the poet in several verses. If the -*s* were left out in verse 398: "Peres et Saint Espirs," this hemistich would be one syllable short as a consequence. Though hiatus is always possible, our poet was not prone to its frequent use. Consider, for example, the first hemistich of the following verses:

---

1 Gossen, # 63. Cf. Schwan-Behrens, # 333 Rem.
2 The inflectional two case system (excluding the Anglo-Norman dialect) remained practically intact until well into the thirteenth century. See P. Studer's edition of *Le Mystère d'Adam* (Manchester, 1962), p. xlviii.
3 See, for example, laisses IX, XII, XXX, etc.
4 It is clear that *pere* and not *peres* is the author's form in this verse. Otherwise the line would have 13 syllables.

Et sa lampe alumee . . . (v. 15)
D'oyle ki la bone euvre . . . (v. 16)
Bone exemple i puet prendre . . . (v. 25)
Espeuse ot bone et belle . . . (v. 39)
Cortoise ert, preus et sage . . . (v. 145)

Peres is also the author's form in verses 90, 126, 165, 421, etc. Otherwise the first hemistich of these lines would also be lacking one syllable.
It is just as clear that *peres* in verses 28, 72, 132, 669, etc. must be attributed to the scribe. Otherwise these lines have 13 syllables.
Likewise, except for *sire* 993, *hom* 28, 338, *per* 157, *emperere* 883, *ber* 4, 301, the inflectional *-s* is always employed in the nominative singular. In the vocative singular, however, we invariably find *sire* 139, 282, 425, etc.; also *hom* 399.

Personal Pronouns
The personal pronouns give occasion for the following remarks:
Tonic Forms
(a) The classical *ego* occurs either as *je/ge/* or *jo,* with the form *je* predominating: *je vel* 295; *je t'oï demander* 825; *je l'ai fait* 827; etc.; *Et g'irai* 243; *l'autre veu ge garder* 294; *vi ge tant* 948; *Que jo . . . me suis fai amesniers* 403; *Viax quant nos t'apieliemes, jo et t'espeuse gente* 1009; and the obviously incorrect double construction *ceüs sui ge jo en agait* 561.
The form *jo* is the anterior form found in the earliest Picard documents (beginning of the 13th century). *Je* was especially employed as the atonic form, *jo/jou* as the tonic form[5]. The form *jou* is not recorded in our text.
(b) The masculine nominative plural *il* is invariably found without the *s: il* 42, 69, 412, etc. The *s* was added towards the end of the 13th century[6].
(c) As object of a preposition, the 3rd person masculine plural form occurs twice as *iaus* (=MF eux): *aprés iaus* 43; *por iaus* 786. The form *iaus* is Picard. See Phonolgy, Close E., (b).

Atonic Forms
The most salient feature found in our text concerning the atonic personal pronouns is that the Picard-Walloon form *le* for Francien *la*[7] invariably occurs in the accusative singular: *Quant le voit li sains hons* 305 (*le=la dame*); *le tramist* 335 (*le=l'ymage*); *le vit* 338 (*le=l'ymage*); *qui le vist blancoiier* 185 (*le=la virgine*); *gardés le bonement* 222 (*le =la moitié*); *Parler le fist com feme* . . . 521 (*le=l'ymage*); *ne le vet pas mostrer* 844 (*le=la cartre*); *ains ne le peuc voir* 845 (*le=la chartre*); *et d'infer le desfent* 890 (*le=la sainte glise*); *d'amor le nos consent* 892 (*le=la chartre*); *Si le rendi* 898 (*le=la chartre*); *Cil le list* 901

---

5 Gossen, # 64. Cf. Schwan-Behrens, # 321 Rem.
6 Schwan-Behrens, # 322, 3. Cf. Joseph Anglade, *Grammaire Elémentaire de l'Ancien Français* (Paris, 1965), p. 89.
7 Gossen, # 63. Cf. Schwan-Behrens, # 323 Rem.

14

(*le=la chartre*). Cf. definite article where sporadically we do find a mixture of the Picard-Walloon form *le* and Francien *la*.

Note 1: Enclisis of the personal pronoun *le* (masc. and neuter) consistently appears after *se*: *sel prent* 303; *sel treve* 853; *sel prisent* 1125; but *si le* 292; generally after *ne*: *nel vet* 103; *nel puist* 195; *nel vos* 283; *nel puisent* 387; *nel savons* 420; *nel set* 534; *nel puet* 536; *nel sai* 609; but *ne le vi* 833; *ne le puet* 863; and *ne le vet* 930.

The enclitic form is not employed when *le=la* (i. e. feminine): *ne le* 844, 845 (*le=la chartre/cartre*).

We also find *del retenir* 94; and *kil* 57 (=*qui le*). No enclisis occurs, however, after *qui*: *qui le vellent* 174; *qui le conduist* 585; *qui le sert* 700; *qui le sieut* 822; etc. Cf. enclitic forms of the definite article.

Demonstratives

I. Derived from *iste*:
Masculine Forms. (a) Except for the nominative singular forms *cis* 232, 256, 543, 545, 1070; *cist* 34; and *ichis* 826, the OF demonstratives derived from *iste* are used only as adjectives in our text.

The nominative singular forms *cis* and *ichis* are characteristic of Picard-Walloon and are derived from *cist* > *cists (*chists) > cis/ciz (chis/chiz)[8].

(b) In the oblique singular, both *cest/ce* appear with the former predominating: *cest* 239, 1198, 1203, etc.; but *ce* 87, 147, 1201, etc.

Feminine Forms. (a) All demonstratives derived from *ista* are employed as adjectives.

(b) Only two forms with the prosthetic *i* appear in our text: *iceste parole* 301 and *iceste racordance* 1035.

II. Derived from *ille*:
Masculine Forms. (a) Except for *Cil beur* 4, the nominative singular form *cil* is found only as a pronoun: *cil* 25, 547, 1147, etc.

(b) The oblique singular form *cel* 290, 294, 500, etc. (*icel* 638, 781) appears only as an adjective.

(c) The oblique singular form *celui* 9, 101, 339, etc. occurs only as a pronoun.

(d) The nominative plural *cil* 379, 888, 1086, etc. and the oblique plural *ceus* 57, 144, 176, etc. appear only as pronouns.

Feminine Forms. Demonstratives derived from *illa* are recorded thrice as pronouns (nom. sing.): *cele* 256, 275, 303; and twice as adjectives: *cele* 589 (nom. sing.) and *cele* 805 (obl. sing.).

---

8 See Schwan-Behrens, # 331, 2 Rem.

III. Derived from *hoc*:

The neuter demonstrative derived from *hoc* occurs either as *c(h)o/c(h)ou,* or *ce,* with the forms *çou/ce* predominating: *çou* 93, 125, 132, etc.; *ço* 201, 421; *cho* 680; and with prosthetic *i*: *içou* 471; *ichou* 647, 878; *ce* 12, 266, 270, etc.; and with prosthetic *i*: *ice* 1019.

Ço is the anterior form found in the earliest Picard documents. After the middle of the 13th century, only the form *c(h)ou* is recorded. This form is especially employed in an atonic position, but from the very beginning it is in competition with the form *c(h)e,* which was originally tonic, but later became atonic[9].

Possessives

I. Tonic Forms (Possessive Pronouns).

In our text, the present day distinction of adjective from pronoun has not yet fully appeared. Only two examples of the possessives used as pronouns occur: *a la vostre soder* 298 and *por les lor* 786. However, a considerable number of possessive pronouns employed as simple possessive adjectives (e. g. *la soie humilités* 651 = MF *son humilité*) occur after the articles (definite and indefinite) and the demonstratives[10].

(a) with the definite article: *la siuwe orisons* 528 (*siuwe* is the Picard form for *soie*)[11]; *la soie humilités* 651; la soie *humilité* 840; *la soie doçour* 1223; *li siens mortés gerriers* 682; *li vostre repos* 729; *la vostre sanblanche* 989; *la nostre humle proiere* 886; *la nostre balie* 935; *le nostre creator* 1195; *la toie compagnie* 934.

(b) with the indefinite article *un*: *un sien despensier* 759; *un sien capelain* 898.

(c) with the demonstratives *cest* and *cel*: *cest mien castiement* 238; *cel nostre anelet* 294.

Note 1: In the example: *por les lor* 786, tonic close *o* has not broken to *ou/eu.* It also appears without the *-s* which was added towards the end of the 13th century by analogy with the nouns[12].

II. Atonic Forms (Possessive Adjectives).

The atonic forms give occasion for only a few remarks:

(a) The weakened forms *no/vo,* for *nostre/vostre,* are characteristic of the Picard-Walloon dialects[13]: *vo enloiement* 226; *vo cuer* 241; *vo congiét* 281; *no poësté* 419.

---

9 Gossen, # 64, p. 101. Cf. Schwan-Behrens, # 332.
10 See Ed. Faral, *Petite Grammaire de l'Ancien Français* (Paris, 1941), p. 30.
11 See Gossen, # 69 and Phonology, W. Cf. Schwan-Behrens, # 326, 2 Rem.
12 Anglade, p. 92. Cf. Schwan-Behrens, # 328, 2.
13 Schwan-Behrens, # 329, 1 Rem. Cf. Gossen, # 68.

The form *se* (=*sa*) *maisnie* 464 is also Picard-Walloon[14]. Cf. *le=la.*
(b) Except for *lors mains* 1116, the possessive adjective *lor* (masc. and fem.) occurs without the -s: *lor mains* 422, 466.
(c) The feminine forms *ma, ta,* and *sa,* are invariably elided before vowels: *m'arme* 243, 962; *t'amosne* 615; *t'espeuse* 939, 1009; *s'amie* 23; *s'espee* 291; etc.

Relative and Interrogative Pronouns. The relative and interrogative pronouns necessitate only the following comments:
(a) The nominative *qui* is frequently employed in the sense of *celui qui*: *qui la veïst* 1129; *qui s'en peut asier* 1163; *qui le vist blancoïier* 185; etc.
(b) The oblique form *cui* has dative (vv. 7, 48, 663, etc.) and genitive (vv. 2, 244, 523, etc. See [c], below) functions, as well as accusative (101, 952, etc.).
(c) The definite article may appear before *cui*: *la cui euvre fu tant* 2 (=*l'oeuvre de qui; dont l'oeuvre*); *la cui amors ne ment* 244; *la cui euvre est provee* 523. Cf. Tonic forms of the Possessives preceded by the definite article.
(d) No confusion of the pronouns *qui* and *que* occurs in our text.

Verbs. Present Indicative. (a) The fact that our text employs only forms without the analogical -*e* in the first person of -*er* verbs is rather significant. No verbal stems necessitating the helping vowel -*e* occur. Therefore, the 1st person singular is invariably differentiated from the 3rd person singular: *pens/pense; desir/desire;* etc.
(b) Both the -*ons* and *omes* forms are recorded in the present indicative and imperative with the former predominating (for all conjugations): *poons* (pres. ind. 4) 134, 290, 764, etc.; *proions* (imperative 4) 1195, 1210; *faisons* (imp. 4) 1201; etc.; but *somes* (pres. ind. 4) 227, 887, 888; *pensomes* (imp. 4) 229. The form -*omes* is Picard (Walloon also)[15].
(c) Though -*s* begins to appear in the 13th century in the 1st person singular of OF -*re* and -*ir* (noninchoative) type verbs, its use is not generalized until the close of the Middle Ages (15th cent.)[16]. Only forms without -*s* occur in our text: *quier* 158, 283, 616; *fui* 566; *vi* 948; etc. Note, in particular, *reng* 401 (VL* RENDO) under the influence of *preng*, present 1 of *prendre*. Cf. Marie de France, *Eliduc*, v. 673: *Pur ceo preng jeo cunseil de vos.*
(d) The 3rd person singular of -*er* verbs invariably loses its final *t*: *apele; aeure; afie; claime; conforte; couche; crie;* etc. This process took place in the 12th century[17].
Note 1: The form *prendent* 761 (3rd person plural of *prendre*) is Picard, undoubtedly an analogical formation with the Picard *prende* (pres. subj.)[18]. .

---

14 Schwan-Behrens, # 327, 1 Rem. Cf. Gossen, # 67.
15 Gossen, # 78. Cf. Anglade, p. 102.
16 Schwan-Behrens, # 374 and # 363, 1. Cf. Anglade, p. 110.
17 Schwan-Behrens, # 352. Cf. Anglade, p. 102.
18 Gossen, # 80.

Note 2: In *oient* 760, 779, 1099 (AUDIUNT), the inflectional yod has not been lost, but *oent* 370.

Imperfect Indicative
(a) In the imperfect and conditional, our 13th century text consistently employs the *-oie, -oies, -oit,* etc., endings. The *-oie* ending replaced the *-eie* ending in the 12th century[19]. The ending *-oie* counts as two syllables in our text (monosyllabic in the 16th century)[20]: *cuidoie* 945; *vivoie* 1017.
(b) Only two forms of the 1st person plural occur in our text: *apieliemes* 1009 and *aviëns* 1027. The *-iemes* form which is Picard and distinguishes it from the neighboring dialects is by analogy with the endings of *sommes, chantames,* etc.[21].
(c) One classical imperfect survives in our text: *ere* 1005 (imp. 1 of *estre*); *ert* 145, 178, 183, etc. (imp. 3); and *erent* 1180 (imp. 6). Note that tonic free open *e* has not diphthongized to *ie*. Cf. *iert* (synthetic future 3 of *estre*). The form *estoie* replaced *ere/iere* in the 14th century[22].

Future
(a) The presence of the svarabhaktic *e* (in the future and conditional of verbs of the classical 3rd and 4th conjugations whose radical ends in a labial or a supported dental) is characteristic of the Picard dialect (Walloon, Lorraine and Anglo-Norman also)[23]. Only one form, however, occurs in our text: *averons* 453. This is not merely an analogical formation with the future of the 1st conjugation, but also a phonetic tendency. However, the verbs *avoir, savoir,* usually occur as *arai, aras, ara . . .* and *sarai, saras, sara , . . .Doner* also occurs as *donrai,* etc. In our text, both *arai* and *avrai* are recorded.
(b) *Iert* (vv. 71, 273, 274, etc.) is the only OF future form derived directly from the classical form (ERIT) that occurs in our text. Diphthongization of the initial tonic open *e* invariably takes place. Cf. *ere* (imperfect).

Strong preterites in *-ui.* (a) In the first person singular of *pooir, poc* 836, 1022, and *peuc* 845, 1033, are analogical Picard forms with *oc/euc* (pret. 1 of *avoir,* attested in the Chanson de geste: *Aiol et Mirabel*); also *peut* 934 (pret. 3). The form *seut* (pret. 3 of *savoir*) 965 and perhaps 311 is recorded in numerous Old Picard texts[24].
(b) The maintenance of the accented close *e* (which then is umlauted as it should be by the final long *i*) of the weak endings is also characteristic of the

---

19 Schwan-Behrens, # 365. Cf. Anglade, p. 103.
20 Anglade, p. 103.
21 Gossen, # 79.
22 Schwan-Behrens, # 417. Cf. Anglade, p. 133.
23 Gossen, # 74.
24 *Ibid.,* # 72.

Picard dialect though forms without *i* occur in almost all Picard texts[25]. For the purpose of localizing our text, this is of special interest, for this tonic close *e* was regularly lost in Preliterary French and replaced by the *wau* element in all *-ui* type preterites except *volui*. The maintenance of this *i* occurs in the weak preterite forms of *pooir* and *avoir*: *euis* 1011, 1015 (pret. 2); *peuis* 768 (pret. 2); also in the imperfect subjunctive of *avoir, pooir, devoir, savoir, conoistre*: *euist* 171, 187, 920 (3rd pers. sing.); *peuist* 307, 308, 588, etc. (3rd pers. sing.); *deuisse* 946, 1071 (1st pers. sing.); *deuisses* 951, 998, 1000 (2nd pers. sing.); *deuist* 1045 (3rd pers. sing.); *deuissiés* 937, 993 (2nd pers. pl.); *seuisse* 845 (1st pers. sing.); *conneuist* 584 (3rd pers. sing.). Note, in particular, *euwist* 73 (imp. subj. 3 of *avoir*) and *fuise* 1022 (imp. subj. 1 of *estre*) which comes directly from the classical form *fuissem*.

Strong preterites in *-si* and *-i*. The preterites in -ISERUNT invariably occur as *-isent* in our text: *sisent* 157; *asisent* 147; *prisent* 60, 1125; *quisent* 142, 447; etc. This ending is characteristic of the Picard dialect[26].
In Picard (Walloon and Lotharingian also), FECERUNT is found as *fisent*: vv. 153, 693, 1166, etc.
Though forms in *-isrent* (and with the insertion of a glide consonant, *-istrent*, *-isdrent*) are recorded in various Old Picard texts, they are rare[27].

Present Subjunctive
The infix *-c(h)-* is characteristic of the Picard dialect[28]. Only one form, however, occurs in our text: *meche* 783. The infixes *-ge-* and *-gn-* (regular or analogical: *maintigne* 131; *sovegne* 226; *prengne* 345, analogous with *plaigne, ceigne,* etc.; *vegne* 662; etc.) are not proper to the Picard dialect[29] and cannot serve to localize our text. However, the form *prende* (PRENDAT) is Picard. See Present Indicative, Note 1.

Imperative.
A conscious attempt has been made to derive the 2nd person singular imperative form directly from the classical form or its reconstructed VL form (in all conjugations): *gari* 568 (VL* GARI); *detien* 570 (on simple verb TENE). Cf. *Alexis* (MS. L), v. 66: Oz mei pulcele celui tien ad espus (See Foerster & Koschwitz, p. 107). Also *fai* 525, 613, 615, etc. (FAC); *consent* 892 (CONSENTI). However, we do find the *s* in *sers* 611 (SERVIS, not from the CL imperative 2 form *servi* which would have given *serf*).

---

25 *Ibid.*, # 73.
26 Gossen, # 76. Cf. P. Fouché, *Le verbe français. Etude morphologique* (Paris, 1931), pp. 272-273, 288, 299-300, 339, 342-343.
27 Gossen, # 77.
28 Gossen, # 80. Cf. Fouché, pp. 37, 151, 161-162, 205-206.
29 *Ibid.*, # 80.

In the 1st conjugation, all imperative 2 forms are derived from the classical (or VL) form which ended in *-a*: *baille* 892; *maine* 770; *lasque* 892.
Note 1: For the *-omes* ending in the 1st person plural, see Present Indicative, (b).
Past (perfect) Participle. In the Picard dialect, the *-iee* ending of the feminine past participle is reduced to *-ie*[30]: *joncië* 179 (VL* JUNCATA); *laisiés* 563 (LAXATAS).

Infinitive.
Confusion of the infinitive ending *er/ier* occurs in *parlier* 469 (VL* PARAU-LARE); *destorbier* 193, 379, 462, 614, etc. (DISTURBARE); *recovrier* 472 (RECUPERARE); *reprovier* 678 (ECCL. LATIN REPROBARE).

Vocalic Alternation
The differences effected by vocalic alternation are usually maintained in our text though a tendency to regularize the conjugated forms is quite discernible: *proie* (VL PRECAT) 123, 200, 378, etc., instead of the correct phonetic form *prie*; *proient* 733, 1213, for *prient*, to render the stem of these forms identical to the other conjugated forms which appear in our text: *proia* 386; *proiiés* 742; *proions* 1195, 1210; *proirons* 771; *proier* 65, 169, 396, etc. (*prier* is un-recorded). Cf. *Roland*: *priet* and *preir, leier, otreir* (correct phonetic form) with their doublets *prier, liier, otriier*[31].

5. Conclusion

Though *P* shows a mixture of dialect features, the preponderance of Picard characteristics is obvious. It is true that Old Picard shares many of these traits with other dialects. However, sufficient diagnostic characteristics proper to the Picard dialect occur (the ending *-iemes* in the Imperfect Indicative; the verbal and adjectival forms where tonic close *e* + nasal > *ain*; etc.) to conclude that *P* belongs to the Picard dialect.
Likewise, the evidence gathered (especially in the section on Morphology: the presence of the Picard forms: *c(h)o/c(h)ou*; *jo/je*; etc.) suffices to date our base manuscript from the 13th century.

---

30 Gossen, # 8. Cf. Anglade, p. 105.
31 See Pope, Chapter IV, Section 8, especially # 927.

I.

Plaist vos a escoter d'un saint home la geste   [125d]
La cui euvre fu tant et saintisme et honeste
C'aprés la morte[1] vie en conquist la celeste?
4   Cil ber soufri por Dieu del siecle la moleste,
Povreté, fain et soif et misere et tempeste,
De cui or font el ciel li saint angle la feste.

II.

Cui Diex a doné sens k'il tort vers moi s'oïe,
8   Et si apoint son cuer a entendre la vie
De celui ki por Dieu soufri tante hascie
Et degerpi en Rome itant grant segnorie
Com vos assés orés, mais k'il soit qui vos die.
12   Ce fu tote s'entente et il n'i fali mie,
Car al regne del ciel vot avoir sa partie.
Primes i a sa voie et sa porte esteblie
Et sa lampe alumee et tos tans bien garnie
16   D'oyle ki la bone euvre qu'il faisoit senefie,
Et en nos vet tos dis qu'il l'ait aparillie
A l'entree de la porte luisant et esclarcie.
Droit cemin tint vers Deu c'ains ne fist departie,
20   Car fois et loiatés qui les autres i guie
Tint tos tans avec soi et porta compagnie.

---

2 c. vie	14 Primes i at sa porte et sa vie e.
4 bor	15 lanterne ardant el chemin esvolie
5 P. et mesaise, f. et s. et t.	16 O *om.*
7 s. za t.	17 Qal encontre lespos li soit aparilhie
8 Et enpoinge s.	18 O *om*
9 hahsiere	19 O *om*
11 Ke v.	20 f. et cariteiz
12 t. sente ne il n.	21 to tens
13 Kil del r.	

4 beur 14 Envers

Virginité la belle, la blance et la florie
Ot tos jors com s'espeuse et maintint com s'amie.
24 Des or mais vos dirons qués en fu la fruie:
Bone exemple i puet prendre cil qui a Deu s'afie!

III.
De Rome fu li sires dont je vos ai contét,
Nés de grant segnorie et de haut pare[n]té.
28 Gentius hom fu ses peres et de grant riceté,
Si com dist li escris u nos l'avons trové.
De trois cens chevaliers le tint on a casé
K'en trestos n'en ot un de si grant povreté
32 Ne portast dras de soie et vers et pailles roés
Et çainture d'orfrois et ermins engoulés.
Eufemïen l'apelle cist qui dist verité,   [126a]
Crestïens fu vers Deu de grant humilité
36 Et sages del siecle, des lois de la cité,
Ne as empereörs n'ot prince plus privé
Ne de plus haut consel, ne de tel dignité.
Espeuse ot bone et bele et de grant net[e]é;
40 Maint an furent ensanble par la Deu volenté,
En foi et en amor et en grant loiaté,
Qu'il ainc n'orent enfant, si lor fu destiné,
Que aprés iaus fust sires de lor grant erité
44 Selonc lor haut linage et lor nobilité.
Et quant Diex ne lor done, molt en sont contristé,
Mais de sa grant merci ne sont pas desperé:
De Sarra lor ramenbre por estre erité
48 Cui Dex dona un fil en son derain aé,
De cui fu li linages dont assés est parlé
Del fil saint Israël, de David le sené,
De la virgine Marie qui ot si grant bonté
52 Que Diex en dagna naistre qui le mont a savé,

---

22 O *om*   36 sages hom d.
23 O *om*   42 Ke ainc . . . fut ordine
24 la finie   43 Ki empres eaz f.
25 en D.   47 r. de sa sterilite
26 donc j. v. a. mostre   49 f. la linie d.
28 richee   50 Des saint I.
30 t. mile serjanz   51 M. et de sa g.
32 soie, vert, vermelh u roe 52 Donc cil Deus deniat n.
34 cil quin d. la v.

D'Elysabeth la vielle, Zacharie le barbé,
Par cui Diex commencha sainte crestïenté
Et selonc son batesme a le mont renovelé.
56 Quant voient qu'autre fois i a Dex si ouvré
Par le merite ceus kil servirent a gré,
El service de Dieu ont tot lor cuer usé
Qui trestote nature mue a sa volenté.
60 Saint esperance i prisent, s'i sont molt conforté,
Car de Dieu a servir sont molt entalenté,
De faire grans amosnes ne [se] sont pas oublïé.
A glises et a povres font molt grant largeté,
64 De messe cascun jor ne sont aseüré,
De proier nuit et jor se sont molt ahané;
De juner, de vilier se sont tant fort pené
Que tot en sont lor vis paile et descoulouré.
68 Mais Diex li bons, li pius ne l'a pas refusés
Le service qu'il font de cuer par verité,
Car selonc lor proiere lor a un fil doné
Qui tant fu sainte cose c'a paine iert raconté.
72 Plus grant joie ot li peres le jor k'il le vit né   [b]
Que s'on l'euwist tot droit de l'empire fievé.
Ses mains tendi al ciel, de joie en a ploré,
En plorant en mercie le haute deïté;
76 Car voit que son service nen a pas dejeté.
Puis fist metre l'enfant sor un porpre listé,
A mostier l'en porterent, si l'ont Dieu presenté,
Et puis del saint baptesme crestïen consecré;
80 Alexis l'apelerent, ensi l'ont confermé.
La prist le jor li enfes vers Dieu estableté,

---

53 vielhe, de Z.   67 descoret
53.1 De saint Hohan, lor fil, ki tant ot   68 nen at p.
      demore   69 Lor s. . . . et en v.
54 sa crestianite   72 l. j. cant lo v.
55 Et segon . . . renove   73 del regne assegureit
56 f. at ja D.   74 Tendit s. m.
57 c. qui s. en g.   75 h. majesteit
58 O om   76 Kor v.
59 Et q. tote n.   77 f. prendre lenfant en u.
60 Grande e. . . . sen s.   79 Puis lont el s.
64 assegureit   80 issi lont
65 n. et di   81 e. sa promiere bonteit

81 estabilite

Bien i sont li parin de lor foi aquité,

Car puis se maintint si tos jors en honesté

84 Com cil cui saint Espirs ot le cuer alumé.

Bone fu la doctrine dont il a escolé,

Car a service Dieu ot tos jors son pensé.

Or commenche la vie de ce boneüré,

88 Comment il a vers Dieu et vers le siecle erré.

IV.

Quant li enfes fu tés que il le pot soufrir,

Li peres le fist bien com a sa loi vestir;

A escole l'envoie por des letres oïr

92 Et des letres aprendre et son sens esbaudir

Por çou que il miex sace Dieu connoistre et jehir;

Et li enfes se paine tos tans del retenir

Çou dont il le puist miex honorer et servir

96 Et de son cors demaine droit sacrefise offrir,

Ses comans a entendre et sa loi a emplir.

La grans amors de Dieu li fait si eslaidir

Tote l'onor del siecle quanke il i puet coisir,

100 Tot li sanble folie quanke il voit bastir.

Molt tient celui a fol cui i voit orgilir

D'onor qu'il ne pora a tos jors maintenir.

En son cuer a pensé, mais nel vet descovrir

104 Por corecier son pere et sa mere marir,

Que il trestot le siecle vet a laron gerpir

Et cast[e]é garder et carité tenir

Et foit et esperance et comans Dé tenir

108 Et tot enpoindre a Dieu son cors et son espir.

Puis c'ot pasé dis ans, garda soi de mentir,

Tot departoit as povres quank'il pooit tenir.

Leus li vint tés novele qu'il ne vosist oïr,

---

82 B. en s.

84 at l.

85 donc il lat e.

91 A lescole . . . p. les livres o.

93 et servir

94 t. jors

95 il poust m. D. ameir e.

97 Et s. c. atendre e. s. l. acomplir

98 Li g.

99 s. kant kenz i p.

83 puist   107 de c.

100 f. cant kenz i v.

101 f. quil i v.

102 Lonor quil at t. j. ne porat m.

103 m. il n. v. gehir

106 g. et toz jors maintenir

107 O *om*

109 O *om*

110 O *om*

111 Puis l.

Car ses peres li rices qui molt a a baillir   [c]
Li vet doner mollier et de s'onor saisir.

V.

Or voit Eufemïens de son fil la valor
Qui si croist en biaté, en bonté, en vigor;
116   De tote honeste gent le tient on a millor
Qui soit en tote Rome del grant jusqu'el menor.
Pui[s] le voient et sage et large doneör
Et a la povre gent respondre par amor;
120   Mais porheuc en son cuer maine si grant labor
Que peu pase de jors ne voist en un destor.
A orison se couche et a larme et a plor,
Dieu proie de bon cuer par sa vraie douchor
124   Qu'il de mort le defende, qu'il ne caie en error,
Que de çou c'a promis ne boist son creator.
Li peres se recorde, mort sont si ancissor,
De cui il a sa terre, sa ricoise francor;
128   Ne il n'a que cel fil, si pense et nuit et jor
Que mollier li donra que pora belisor
Et de plus haut linage et de plus douce amor,
Dont Diex li doinst tel fruit qui maintigne s'onor.

VI.

132   Quant çou entent li peres, si commence a penser,
Aglaël, sa mollier, le prent a raconter:
»D'Alexi, nostre fil, que molt poons amer,
A lui pens des or mais; i a biel baceler,
136   Querre li vet mollier et ma terre doner.«
La mere quant l'entent, jus se laise avaler,
As piés li va, de joie si commence a plorer:
»Sire,« ce dist la dame, »Diex t'en puist conforter

---

112 Ke . . . q. m. sen pot joir	122 O *om*
113 volt	123 O *om*
113.1 Et trestote sa terre faire a lui obeir	124 Ke del mont lo garisse
114 Quant v.	125 Et de ce kait p.
115 Q. toz c. e. bonte, e. bealte, e. v.	127 forzor
116 h. lo t.	128 at mais denfanz, s.p. nuit e.
118 v. sage e.	132 Q. ensi ot l. p. afichiet son penseir
119 par dulzor	133 la pris
120 Mai p. . . . m. tant g.	135 Ai penseit d.
121 j. ke il a Deu ne plor	138 A. p. len v.
129 besisor	

140   Que la nostre lignie puist par lui raviver.«
        Or ne s'atargent mais de lor plait a mener,
        Tel pucele li quisent qui molt fait a loier
        En totes les manieres c'om i vet demander,
144   Del lignage un de ceus qui Rome ot [a] garder;
        Cortoise ert, preus et sage, so ciel n'avoit son per.
        Li parent d'ambes pers les font entrafïer,
        Puis asisent un jor por ce pla[i]t afiner
148   Et por le haut linage venir et asambler.
        Le jor i ot grant joie quant vint a l'espouser,
        Partot puet on oïr ces vïeles soner,
        Harpes, rotes et lires et frestraus demener,   [d]
152   Giges soner en haut, canteörs orgener.
        Devant saint Boneface les fisent coroner,
        Selonc la loi de Rome les ont fait ajoster,
        Beneïr et sanier, loiament espouser.
156   Puis font par le païs cent cierges alumer,
        As maistres dois se sisent li demaine et li per.
        Tant fu rices li plais ne vos en quier fauser,
        N'i fali nule riens quanke on puet penser.
160   A grant joie ont le soir receü le souper,
        Mais asés aront duel le matin a disner,
        Tote revertira lor grant joie a plorer.

        VII.
        Le soir i ot grant joie as noces commencier
164   Quant des dois sont levé li baron chevalier;
        Li peres fu cortois, n'i ot que ensegnier,
        De la gent et du peule fait le maison vuidier;
        Puis commande Alexin, son fil, qu'il voist couchier
168   En la cambre o la virgine, s'en face sa mollier.
        Li dansias quant l'entent, ne s'en fait pas proier,

---

140 l. par lui puist r.   155 l. consecreir
141 atargent mie   156 lo palais
143 mesures cum ja v.   157 A. m. d. lenguient cil d. et cil p.
144 Del lin lempereor q. R. at a. g.   158 q. fabler
145 O om   159 r. cant com pot desireir
146 O om   162 ravertistrat
147 lor plait   164 cil b.
148 E. par lur h.   166 fist lo palais v.
149 Lo soir   167 fil, ke v.
150 v. canteir   169 fist
151 Rotes, harpes et lires e.

Car molt crient en son cuer son pere a corechier.
En la cambre s'en entre, mais il euist plus chier

172 A estre outre la mer a la loi d'amosnier
Et si povres d'avoir qu'il fust a mendiier.
Sa maisnie en re[n]voie qui le vellent descaucier,
Dist ne vet que ja hons soit a son despoulier;

176 Seus remest en la cambre, ceus ens fi[s]t repairier.
La cambre fu molt gente si com por tel mestier,
Portendue ert de pailes et de flors d'olivier,
Joncïé fu par terre de fuelles de lorier,

180 De roses et de lis i ot plus d'un sestier
Et de rices espeses por l'oudor enforcier,
Molt fesist a autre home le coraige eshaucier;
Et li lis ert tant rices et tant fait a proisier,

184 Ne vos en sai les los ne le pris desraisnier.
Et la virgine ert tant belle, qui le vist blancoiier
El lit u elle atent son forceur desirier,
Molt euist cuer de piere u de fer u d'acier

188 Cui ne presist talent del siecle a asaiier.
Mais Alenxis, li enfes, a pris tel consillier
Qu'il n'i vet pas son cuer torner ne apoiier.   [127a]
Devant a pavement se va agenoullier,

192 A la terre se couche, Dieu commence a huchier
Que la nuit le garisse de si fort destorbier,
Del siecle dont il tant se voloit escacier

---

171 En c. sen vait
172 Estre
173 Issi p.
174 quil v.
175 j. soit h. a se d.
176 S. remeist ot la virgene, . . . repairir
177 a t.
178 P. de p. e. d. rais d.
180-186
   Li liz par fut tant riches et tant fist a prisier,
   Ne vos en sai lo pris ne lo los desrainier;
   De tantes bones speces font lodor enforcier,
   Mut feist a altre home lo corarage haitier;
   Et la virgene ert tant bele, qui la veist blanchier
187 c. d. fier u de pierre u
188 a ensaier
190 aploier
191 sen v.
194 s. ke il t. soi voit encaciier

186 forceus   192 la se t.

27

Que li cuer ne li mente ne nel puist engignier.
196   Or pense li saint enfes, trop se puet atargier,
Que fuir l'en convient et la terre vuidier,
Se il se vet del siecle garir ne delaier.

VIII.

Li enfes en la cambre desor le pavement
200   Proie Dieu et aeure, molt pleure tenrement.
Molt par est anguoseus selonc ço que il sent,
Car s'il s'en fuit de Rome, bien set a ensïent,
Grant duel fera son pere et sa mere ensement;
204   Mais de cel Ewangile li ramembre sovent
Que cil treuve lisant qui des letres entent,
Si comme Diex parole et castoie sa gent:
Qui plus aime ne pere ne mere ne parent,
208   Fil ne mollier ne terre, honor ne casement
Que moi, dist nostre Sires, ne mon commandement,
Il n'est dignes de moi ne a moi ne s'atent.
Saint Alexins i pense del cuer parfondement,
212   Atant s'est sus levés, molt s'afice forment,
A pere ne a mere n'avra mais son entent,
Tot le mont gerpira, Dieu prendra a garant.
Devant le lit s'asist sor un siege d'argent,
216   Les chiés de sa çainture trenche isnelement
Et si prist son anel tot porpenseëment;
A l'espee le trenche, l'une moitiét en prent,
Torna vers la pucelle, si l'en fist un present.
220   "Recevés," fait il, "belle, par droit confortement,
Les ciés de ma çainture et de mon anel gent
Vos doinst l'une moitié, gardés le bonement,
Et je garderai l'autre acoragïement.
224   Belle suer, membrés vos de vostre espousement,
Por Dieu vos pri, le voir, a vivre castement
Et que il vos sovegne de vo enloiement
Comment somes ensamble par le saint sacrement;

---

195 m. nil nel p.	206 O *om*
196 s. hom	208 Ne t. ne m., onor n.
197 A f.	210 Non est d.
198 n. delacier	211 O *om*
200 a., priet m. t.	217 Et at pris s. a. mut p.
202 R., ce s.	218 O *om*
203 m. et sa gent	220 confermement
205 O *om*	

228 Or nos [j]oingnons a Dieu par bon entendement,
De bien faire pensomes, de vivre justement. [b]
Cis siecles est molt faus, plains de favoiement,
Vils est et decevables, mortés a tote gent;
232 Perileus, decevables, fols est cis qui s'i prent;
Sa ricoise et s'onor et son deduitement,
La joie que il mostre revient a plorement;
Cil qui trop s'i aise torne a destruitement,
236 Car la joie del ciel pert pardurablement
Et prent sans fin ostel en infier le puslent.
Bele suer, car creés cest mien castiement,
Des vises de cest siecle ayés astinement,
240 Dieu espeuse soiés, si errés loiament,
Cascun jor en vo cuer aiés ramenbrement
Del grant espeus celeste qui el ciel nos atent.
Et g'irai saver m'arme, se Dex le me consent,
244 Et Diex vos doinst bien faire la cui amors ne ment,
Del pechié nos garise qui tot le mont sosprent;
Et Diex quant jugera le siecle a jugement
Nos doinst ensanble glorie, el ciel herbrigement."
248 Quant la pucelle l'ot, ne li respont noient
A quanke il a dit, ains i pense forment;
Cast[e]é a tenir li enfes li aprent,
De devine escripture bias sermons li despent.
252 Tot sanble esperiteus, n'a del siecle talent,
Molt se met en grant paine, tot cange son jovent.

IX.
Es les vos en la cambre ambes deus enfermés,
Tot droit devant le lit se seent lés a lés,
256 Se cele fu honteuse, et cis fu plus assés.
Li bers saint Alexins fu forment trespensés,
Ne set que il puist faire, tant par est esgarés;
Por çou que il estoit des letres bien fondés
260 Et que il set del siecle et de Dieu les decrés,
Crient ke tel rien ne face dont tos jors soit gabés;

221-253
Del grant espos celeste qui en ciel vos atent (242)
Ke Deus soit entre nos, la cui amurs ne ment (244)
Del pechiet vos garisse qui tot lo mont sorprent (245)
Puis sen vait de la cambre mut esploitosement (245.1)
Mut soi met en grant paine, tot change son jovent (253)

Molt porpense et engigne comment soit desevrés,
Bien set en son corage qu'il en sera dampnés
264 Se de sa cast[e]é est or si deflorés
Qu'il promist a garder, ja ert lons tens passés.
Quant ce vint a grant pieche qu'il fu bien porpensés,
Si regarda s'espeuse et dist: »Or m'entendés,
Bele, tres ciere amie, por Dieu car me creés,   [c]
Cis siecles est mavais, si comme vos savés,
Et cascun jor enpire, ce est la verités.
Prometés Damredieu que tant com vos vivrés
272 Par moi ne par autrui vostre virginités
N'iert enfrente a nul jor; bon leuvier en avrés,
Car o les autres virgines iert vos ciés coronés.«
Cele dist: »Volentiers, si com vos commandés,
276 Mais que vos ensement autretel me tenés.«
Ce dist saint Alexins: »Donkes le m'afiés.«
»Volentiers,« ce dist elle, »or endroit le prenés.«
Il le prent et la soie li rafie delés.
280 Quant les fois sont donees, Alexins s'est levés
Et a dit a s'espeuse: »Vo congiét me donés!«

X.
»Sire,« ce dist s'espeuse, »u volés vos aler?«
»Bele,« ce respont il, »nel vos quier a celer,
284 En une estragne terre por mon cors deserter;
Car en saint Ewangile oï saint Jehan conter,
Qui trestout ne laira por Damredieu amer,
Pere et mere et enfans et sa bone per
288 Et parens et avoir, ne se pora saver
Ne el regne del ciel avec Dieu habiter.
Poons nos en nul sens cel commant trespasser?«
Puis a prise s'espee por son anel coper;
292 Quant l'ot parmi copé, si le prist a mostrer.
»Bele, l'une moitié vos vel or commander
De cel nostre anelet, l'autre veu ge garder,
Et quel part que je voise, je vel o moi porter.
296 Ne ja mar creés home, vielart n'a baceler,
Que il mort m'ait veü n'a terre ne a mer,
S'il ne puet ceste piere a la vostre soder;
Ne ja n'en aiés cure a amer n'a parler
300 Por cose c'om vos puist prometre ne doner.«

---

264 ore   266 g. piechie

30

A iceste parole saint Alexins li ber
S'en est alés vers l'uis, qu'il le vot deffremer,
Quant cele li ceurt sus, sel prent a acoler,
304   Entre ses bras la dame se commenche a pasmer.
Quant le voit li saint hons, si commenche a plorer,
Ja veïsiés tel duel quant vint a desevrer;
Il n'a sou siel nul home tant peuist sermoner   [d]
308   Qui vos desist awan, tant se peuist pener,
Le duel qu'ele demaine quant l'en voit aler.

XI.
Or s'en va li dansias, n'i vet plus demorer,
Et vint a son tresor la u il seut aler;
312   Tant prist de son tresor que il en puet porter.
Puis est partis de Rome, n'i vet mais demorer,
Tote nuit ne fina dans Alexins d'aler
Et le jor el demain ne vot ainc arester.
316   Tot droit a port de Caples est entrés en la mer
En une nef garnie qui s'en devoit passer
Outre el regne de Syre por avoir acater.
Tant keurent nuit et jor par oscur et par cler
320   C'al droit port a Landise entré sont en la mer.
Assés ara ses peres des or mais a plorer
Et sa mere et s'enspeuse plaindre et adoloser.

XII.
Quant li saint enfes fu fors de la nef issus,
324   La nuit vi[n]t a Landise, el main s'en est issus;
Tost s'en fuit de la vile qu'il n'i soit coneüs
Et trespase de Syre tertres et puis agus.
Tant va par ses jornees qu'il ne fu retenus,
328   C'an pangne et a travall est a Hrohais venus,
La trova une ymage dont Diex fait grans vertus.

254-309
    O *om*
310 ni v. mais d.
311 vait a. s. t. u i. soloit a.
312 s. avoir cum i. e. volt p.
313 volt giens d.
314 O *om*
315 O *om*
317 q. se d.
319 jor et nuit p.

320 L. font lor nef arriveir
321 peres qui mut lo puet ameir
322 e. sa spouse des or mais a ploreir
323 fut d. l. n. descenduz
324 O *om*
325 T. soi part de Landize q.
326 s. et valz et p.
327 j. kainc n.
329 ymagene donc D. fist g.

XIII.

Es vos dant Alexin dedens Rohais entrés,
La trova une ymage de grant atorité

332   Del fil Dieu Jhesu Crist qui siet en maiesté;
Si com li ancisor le vos on[t] raconté,
Ainc ne fu faite d'ome carmement engenré.
Li fix Dieu le tramist un roi de la cité,

336   Abagarons ot non de si grant dignité
Com li escris raconte u nos l'avons trové.
Quant li saint hom le vit, Dieu en a aouré;
Or pense de celui que Diex li a mostré

340   Ne s'en movra en pieche selonc sa volenté.
Mais icis Ewangiles li est molt en pensés
Que Diex a ses desciples a dit et confermé:
Qui vet suiier ma trache de cuer par verité

344   Soi meïsmes renoit, richoise et poësté,
Et si prengne sa crois et si ait povreté.
Quant il voit que li povre sont si boneüré,   [128a]
Que Diex lor a doné si grant benignité,

348   Povres desire a estre tot por [sa] saveté.
Dont regarde vers Dieu, si a molt souspiré
De l'avoir que il a avec soi aporté,
Se tient molt envers Dieu de pechié encombrés.

352   Trestot l'a leus vendu, cangié et desborsé,
Puis l'a doné as povres par si grant largeté
C'ainc n'en retint o soi un denier monaé.
O les autres mendis s'est mis tot de son gré;

356   Or a ensi vers Dieu son cuer aseüré,
Nel i vera mais hons trescangié ne müé.
D'un diemenche a autre a son tens ordené,
Reçoit corpus domini par grant humilité;

360   De juner, de vilier a si son cors pené
Que taint en a le vis, paile et descoulouré.
Ja n'iert mais reconus en trestot son aé

---

330 saint A.
335 D. la t.
336 ot a n.
338 si at D. a.
339 p. dicel liu ke D.
342 O *om*
343 c. et en veteit.
347 Cant D. l. a. d. issi g. fealteit
347.1 Ke lo regne del ciel lur at abandoneit

348 O *om*
349 Puis r. v. soi si
352 lat lors v.
356 issi v.
358 diemege
359 Kil r.
360 De voilier, de juneir ait si
361 Ke tant e. a. l. v. taint et d.
362 m. coneguz

335 D. Jhesu Christ l.   346 Q. li v.   348 desires

A pere ne a mere ne a serjant privé.

XIV.

364   Or est saint Alexins a Rohais com mendis;
       Grant duel en a en Rome a trestos ses amis,
       Quant il par la cité l'ont tant cercié et quis
       K'il ne sevent vreté vers quel part il s'est mis.
368   Li peres le fait querre par tot l'ample païs
       Et par terre et par mer et par nuis et par dis.
       Quant n'en oent novele si se claime caitis,
       Ja n'en ara mais joie ensi l'a entrepris
372   Desci que il sara s'il est u mors u vis.

XV.

       Molt est dolans li peres, n'i a que corechier,
       Quant il nen ot novele de son grant destorbier.
       Atant de ses serjans com il vot atirier,
376   De tos ses milors homes qui molt l'avoient chier
       Le fist par tot le monde et quere et cerchier,
       Si lor proie por Dieu molt fort a esploitier.
       Cil en passent la mer sans nesun destorbier,
380   Puis se metent a terre, n'i velent atargier
       Par le regne de Sire tot le cemin plenier,
       Sont venu a Rohais, droit devant le mostier
       Troverent lor signor u tenoit un sautier.
384   Il les connut molt bien quant les vit aprochier,
       Le cief bronca vers terre et si se tra[i]st arier,   [b]
       Et proia Dieu del ciel qui de tot puet aidier
       Que coinoistre nel puisent si pere mesagier.
388   Tant a la char penee de son cors travilier,
       De juner et d'orer, de pener, de vilier
       Que tote sa sanblanche li fait si fort cangier,
       Ja n'iert mais conneüs ne l'en estuet gaitier

363.1 Fresci ke en son regne laurat
       Deus coroneit
364–372
      O *om*
373 ni ot ke
374 g. deseier
377 e. requerre e. c.
378 Et s. l. p. mut p. D. del e.

372 u l v.   374 noet n.

379 C. soi p. . . . negon d.
380 ver t.
383 son sanior
384 tres b.
385 Son c.
386 E. priet Damrideu q.
388 car mueie
389 paime et de v.

392	A pere ne a mere, n'a serjant n'a mollier.
	L'amosne li donerent com a autre asmosnier.
	Quant il a receüe, molt se prist a haitier,
	Damredieu en aeure qui tot a a jugier
396	De çou c'as sers son pere li lait le pain proier.

XVI.

»Biax peres, Jhesu Cris, voirs Diex en trinité,
Peres et Saint Espirs, trinus en unité,
Vrais Diex et parfais hom qui le mont as savé,
400 Racine de tot bien et confors de bonté,
Grasses te reng et los de tot mon bon pensé
De çou que ta pietés a si en moi ouvré
Que jo a sers mon pere qui sont de m'erité
404 Me sui fai[s] amesniers por toi tot [de] mon gré;
Se il ne m'en connurent, de ce m'est plus amé.«
Avec les autres povres s'en va par la cité
A l'amosne proier de la Dieu carité.

XVII.

408 Li serjant se rapairent quant ne l'ont ravisé.
Tant l'ont par tote tere et quis [et] demandé
Que lor drap nuef et fort sont viés et depané.
Ariere se repairent dolent et abosmé
412 Et plorant et irié quant il ne l'ont trové.
Trestot par autre voie qu'il ne soient torné
Sont repairié a Rome tot confus et tot lasé.
Content a lor segnor tot com il ont alé
416 Et cercië la terre et en lonc et en lé
Dechi k'en Babyloiene el regne defaé,
K'il n'i a port de mer ne pont sor flun levé
Nos tot enquis n'aions selonc no poësté;

392	a s.	407	az almones
394	Q. i. lat r., m. sen p.	408	L. s. sen returnent
396	Cant il a.	411	sen r.
397	B. sires	412	E. dolant et irous
401	d. trestot mon p.	413	n. fuissent t.
402	pitiez	414	et l.
403	as serjanz.	417	Fresci k.
405	Ne i. n. moi conoissent	419	Nen aient t. e. s. lor p.
405.1	Puis soi retrast arriere, sait lo chief enclineit		

392 ne s. 405 amer

420	Nel savons mais u querre, tot en sons desperé.
	Li peres quant ço voit n'en sara verité,
	Entre lor mains se pasme, tant a le cuer iré.
	Molt se claime caitis, dolans et maleürés, [c]
424	A ambes mains detrait sa barbe a poil meslé.
	»Biax Sire, Damredieu, vrais rois de maiesté,
	Comment l'a[i] je perdu? Ja le m'avois doné.«
	»Dolante,« dist la mere, »peciés le m'a enblé.«
428	Sanglente sa maisele, son cainse depané,
	Deronpue sa crisne, son cief escevelé,
	Se gaimente et dolouse, com ait cuer desevré;
	Molt sovent i regrete les sens et la biaté
432	Que Diex a mis en lui et la grant honesté.

XVIII.

	»Biax fix,« ce dist la mere, »com or sui constritee!
	En quel dolor as mis ta mere l'esgaree!
	Ja mais tant com je vive ne serai confortee,
436	Ne ne vestirai porpre ne ma ciere lavee,
	Mais en sac et en cendre plorai ma destinee
	Qui si tost m'est falie et ah noi[ent] tornee.«
	»Amis,« ce dist s'espeuse, »com m'avés desperee,
440	Molt par a vostre joie trop corte la dure[e]
	C'onques l'amors de vos ne fu vers moi privee,
	Mais si virgene pucele com sui de mere nee
	Serai de vif mari veve feme clame[e].«

XIX.

444	Es vos molt grant le duel et le plor et le cri
	A pere et a la mere qui l'avoient nori
	Et a sa gente espeuse qui nel mi[st] en obli.
	Puis s'en vont en la cambre, c'ainc n'i quisent respi,

420 N. sevent . . . en sunt d.
424 barba
426 maus tu d.
427 Chaitive . . . jal ma p. e.
428 ses mameles
429 sa scrine, s. c. desceveleit
430 cuer forsenet
431 lo sens
435 Juer m.
436 p. niert m.
447 aint

436.1 Ne mes cors acehmeiz ne ma
    chambre pareie
437.1 De la grant esperance que Deus
    mavoit donee
439 sa spouse
440 nostre j. eut curte dureie
442 c. fui
446 met
447 cambre quil ni mistrent r.

<pre>
448   N'i la[i]sierent de biel, cordine ne tapi,
       Ne paille ne orfrois ne cendal ne sami;
       Tote le despoulierent comme liu en erbi.
       Par tot jeterent cendre, puis si ont establi
452   Que ja mais en lor vies ne giront en un lit,
       Ne averont ensanble nesun carnel delit.
       L'espeuse en jure Dieu qui Tobïe gari
       Et Sarram conforta et castïa David
456   Que ja mais compagnie n'ara d'autre mari.
       En la cambre demaine u de li departi
       Atendra mais o duel Alexin son ami
       Desque la verité en avra desenti
460   Se il est mors u vis u revenra a li.

       XX.
       Molt demaine grant duel le viex o sa mollier   [d]
       De lor fil c'ont perdu, de lor grant destorbier.
       Tel duel en a s'enspeuse tote cuide esragier;
464   Se maisnie le pleurent qui molt l'avoient chier,
       N'i a celui ne pleure ne se puet rehaitier,
       Molt detordent lor mains, si prenent a huchier:
       »Biax Sire, Jhesu Cris, com nos avés abaisiés!
468   Por coi nos a[s] tolu le millor consellier
       Qui soit remés en Rome et le plus bel parlier?
       Nus ne puet sa bonté el mont aparilier.«
       Mais içou que lor vaut? Quant tot a mis arier
472   La ricoise del mont, n'i ont mais recovrier,
       Car il est a Rohais a guise de paumier;
       A loi de peneant siet devant le mostier,
</pre>

<pre>
448 l. dossal, cortine n.   462 g. deseier
450 liu enermit   463 en fait le. t. en quide e.
451 si sunt e.   464 plangnent
452 Mais en tote l. v.   465 Celui ni at n. p. cum nel puet r.
453 Ne naverons e. negon c.   467 B. s., Damrideus, c. n. vus abaissier
454 Lespose j.   468 toloit
456.1 Anz ratendrat celui dont at lo cuer   469 Et lo plus dulz sanior et lo plus
      marrit   droiturier
457 d. la u derrains lo vit   472 d. secle
458 O om   473 dalmonier
459-460
     Fresci quele saurat sil est mors u il vit

453 averons   465 puent
</pre>

Le cief baise vers terre por son cors travilier.
476 La proie nuit et jor por le mont esclarier,
Por les peciés del siecle qu'il voit montepliier,
Que Diex sa creature garisse d'encombrier
Et des mavais engiens a felon avresier,
480 Qu'al grant jor de juïse quant Diex venra jugier
En paradys celeste se puissent herbrigier.

XXI.

A Rohais est li sires si com avés oït,
Grant duel en a en Rome et grant plor et grant crit.
484 Le deduit de sa terre a tos mis en oblit
Et son pere et sa mere qui l'avoient nouri
Et sa mollier la gente ainc plus bele ne vi;
S'onor et tos ses homes qui por lui sont mari,
488 Tot a por Dieu amor et laisiét et gerpi,
En juner, en orer a torné son deli.
Del pain que on li done mangue assés peti,
Ains le depart as autres sens nesun contredi;
492 Plus n'en retient o soi ne mais c'a paines vit,
Car il le fait por Dieu, bien li sera meri.

XXII.

Es vos dant Alexin a Rohais com frarin,
Ne porte mantel vair ne peliçon ermin
496 Ne bliaut ne cendal ne cemise de lin;
Mais la haire vestue, descaus piés a tapin
Seit devant le mostier a loi de pelerin.
Les amosnes mangue mais ne gouste de vin;
Cel commant d'Ewangile tient sovent a voisin   [129a]
Que on trueve lisant e[n] un livre devin,
Et par nuit et par jor est en grant desiplin,
S'il a hui a mangier ne pense del matin,
504 N'amontiant pas deniers ne argent ne or fin.

---

476 n. e. di p. l. m. resplaidier
480 del
483 a R.
486 kainc belisor n.
487 Son o. et s. h.
490 lom l. d. manjoit a.
491 Az . . . negun c.
492 s. mais tant ka paine en v.
493 Mais sil l.

494 saint A.
496 b. de cendal
497 Ot sa h.
499 manjout ne ne g.
500 Cel precept
501 O *om*
502 O *om*
503 Qui ui at a m. gard ne pens d.
504 Nassemblet

Tot çou que on li done la u il siet el cemin
Rent si as autres povres, n'en retient romoisin
S'en n'est por sostenanche de son cors le frarin.

XXIII.

508   Entre la gent del siecle de pechié enbrasee,
     A Rohais la cité outre la mer salee,
     En itel penitanche com avés escoutee
     Estuit saint Alexins en sa vie privee
512   Dis et set ans entiers c'ainc n'en fali jornee
     Que n'i fu sa bontés a home revelee.
     Mais isi grant lumiere qu'en lui ert alumee
     Ne puet mie estre a long sous le mont escoutee;
516   Et quant Diex ne vet mais qu'ele soit plus celee,
     S'en fist tel demostrance qui asés fu provee.
     Une ymage molt belle ert el mostier posee
     El non saint Marie et faite et figuree,
520   Por l'amor al saint home l'a Diex enluminee,
     Parler le fist com feme qui fust vive et senee.
     Le sougretain apele un main a l'ajornee:
     »Va quere le saint home la cui euvre est provee,
524   El ciel o les saint angles est sovent recordee;
     Fai le entrer el mostier sans nule demoree,
     Bien est dignes qu'il ait de paradis l'entree,
     Et la porte del ciel li est abandonee,
528   Car la siuwe orisons est a Dieu tant amee,
     Plus li rent bone odor que n'est mirre enbrasee;
     Saint Espirs est en lui par cui s'arme iert savee.«

---

505 lom
507 Mais par la s. d. s. c. l. mechin
507.1 Et proiet a Damrideu et tient
     lo chief enclin
507.2 Kil ait mercit del pople cant li monz
     prendrat fin
508-511
     En itel penitance cum aveiz esculteie
     Estiet sainz Alexis en sa vie priveie
     A Rohais, la citeit, ultre la meir saleie,
     Al chief dinde, la grant, en estrani contreie
529 ront

512 ans toz plains c.
515 pot . . . mui absconseie
516 nel volt m. kele fust p.
518 b. fut
519 E. n. la mere Deu e.
520 Par amur . . . lait D.
522 un jor
523 c. vie e. loeie
528 sue
529 ke soit m.

XXIV.

Quant ot li sougretains l'ymage si parler,
532 Merviliés s'en est molt, Dieu commenche a loer;
Puis ist fors del mostier, n'i vet plus demorer,
Le saint home va quere mais nel set raviser   [129b]
Ne conoistre par vis ne des autres sevrer.
536 El mostier se repaire quant il nel puet trover,
Et vint devant l'ymage, se prist a souspirer;
A la terre se couce joste un marbre piler,
Sovent bat sa poitrine, si commenche a plorer,
540 Et proie Damredieu qui tot a a saver
Qu'il li laist le saint home conoistre et encontrer.
L'ymage li respont: »Ne t'en caut a douter,
Car cis que tu veras el parevis entrer
544 Et sëoir pres de l'uis et le cief encliner,
C'est cis cui Diex commande en sa glise a entrer.«
Or ne se pora mais saint Alexins celer,
Si tost com cil le voit , se se laise avaler;
548 Les piés li ceurt baisier, si commenche a plorer,
De pitié et d'amor le prist a orer
Que il voist el mostier o les autres ester.
Li saint hons quant l'oï ne li vot pas veer,
552 A sougretain se laise ens el mostier mener.
La novele s'espant qui fait manifester
De lui la bone vie qui tant fait a amer.
Or a Diex sa lumiere fait en haut alumer,
556 Tot le kerent veöir, servir et honorer;
Si grant honor li portent vielart et baceler
Que ne poroie mie la moitiét raconter.

XXV.

Quant voit saint Alexins l'onor que on li fait,
560 De cuer plaint et souspire, molt li parvint a lait.

---

531 cele ymagenc p.
532 O *om*
533 Isi sen f. d. m., que ni volt d.
534 L. s. lome . . . seit u trover
535 vis des
536 sen r. . . . pot
537 si p.
538 O *om*
539 O *om*
540 t. a s.
541 Ke li

543 Icil cui tu v. e. p. esteir
547 cum il lo truevet si s.
549 a conjureir
550 Kil alhet e. mostie
553 L. parole
554.1 Et ke Deus a limagene fist por
      samur parleir
557 S. honor . . . et vielh et b.
558 Ne vos en poroi
559 lom
560 li pervient

»E Diex,« fait il, »merchi! ceüs sui ge en agait
A vil serpent antif qui tos biens contrestait;
Les honors c'ai laisiés me ramaine et ratrait,
564 En l'une main le feu et en l'autre le lait,
De la dolor del siecle me revet metre en plait;
S'or ne fui ceste honor, molt malement me vait.«

XXVI.

»Biax sire, Damrediex,« ce dist saint Alexins,
568 »Gari moi de l'agait a mortel anemis,
De l'engien a serpent qui tant home a malmis,
Detien mon cuer en force a ice grant peril
Que ne soie caüs, engigniés ne sospris.«   [c]
572 Or pense li saint hons et tel consel a pris
Qu'il s'en fuira d'ileuc en un autre païs,
U on nel connistra ne par fais et ne par dis.
Un soir si com la gens se fu en repos mis,
576 Et la cités dort tote et la lune esclarcist,
S'est partis de Rohais c'ainc ne jehi home vis.
Tant va par ses jornees descaus piés et mendis
C'a Landisse est venus, mais ne sai en quel dis.

XXVII.

580 Quant vint saint Alexins a Landisse sor mer,
Ne vet mie en la vile longement demorer;
En une nef s'en entre por a Tarses aler,
A mostier de saint Pol, la voroit arester
Que on nel conneuist tote sa vie user.
Mais Diex qui le conduist en vet el ordener:
Un vens lor est salis qui fait lor nef torner,
Si est entrés es voiles, tantost les fait sigler,

---

561 fai moi m.! c. s. en la.
562 Al viel s. a. q. tot bien c.
563 cai guerpies
564 m. lo miel e.
569 s. entoissiet q.
570 i. kai empris
571 s. engeniez, deceuz ne s.
574 lom . . . f. n. p. vis
575 li gent soi sunt en r.
576 li lune

561 ge jo e.

577 nel gehit amis
577.1 Ne a vielh ne a jovene, na homme
     qui soit vis
578 par lo chemin
579 quanz
581 N. volt mais . . . l. sojorner
585 volt
586 fist la n.
587 Puis est . . . t. la fist s.

588   Saiete ne quariaus ne s'i peuist durer;
          Tant lor dure cele ore par oscur et par cler
          Que droit a port romain les a fait ariver.
          Quant li saint hons fu fors, si prent a esgarder;
592   Le liu, l'estre et la terre commence a raviser,
          Vit la terre de Rome u il seut converser.
          Les iex dreça al ciel, si commence a plorer
          Et jure Damredieu qui tot a a saver
596   Que ja a estragne home ne vora encombrer
          De son cors herbrigier et servir et garder,
          Mais tot droit a son pere qui tant le puet amer
          Ira por l'amor Dieu son hostel demander,
600   Se Diex li done encore vif et sain retrover;
          Car tant est tains et noirs de sa car a pener,
          Ja n'iert mais reconus a sergant ne a per.

XXVIII.
          Or s'en vait li saint hons, n'i vet mais atargier,
604   Entrés est dedens Rome le grant cemin plenier,
          Vai s'ent parmi ces rues a guise de pamier,
          Eufemïen encontre, son pere o le vis fier,
          Del palais se repaire u on soloit pla[i]dier;
608   Aprés son dos le sivent plus de cent chevalier
          Et des autres maisnies tant, nel sai esprisier.
          Li saint hons quant le voit si commence a hucier:
          »Eufemïen, sers Dieu, mon cors ne desprisier,   [d]
          Aiés merchi, por Dieu, de ce povre pamier,
          Fai moi dedens ta cort en un lit herbrigier
          U je ne face a home noise ne destorbier;
          Fai moi doner t'amosne, molt en ai grant mestier,
616   Por l'amors Alexin, biax sire, le te quier,
          Ton fil que tu amoies et tenoies tant chier

---

589 ciste ore
590 r. font la neif antreir
591 prist
594 drezoit
595 a gardeir
597 c. elbrigier ne s. ne g.
598 q. mut lo suet a.
599 p. amur
602 m. coneguz
603 ni volt plus
605 dalmonier

607 lom suet p.
609 E. de laltre mainie t., n. puis desrainier
610 vit
611 despitier
612 A. p. D. m. dicest p.
613 liu
614 ne encombrier
615-617
    Por amur a celui cui avoies plus chier,
    Moi fai doneir talmone, mut en ai grant
    mestier.

Que Diex le laist encore a Rome repairier
Et veöir a tes iex et son cors manoier.«
620 Quant ot Eufemïens le pelerin proier,
Por l'amor Alexin l'ostel et le mangier,
Si li ramembre leus de son grant destorbier.
S'il sospire del cuer, ne me doi mervillier,
624 C'onques puis qu'il perdi le fil de sa mollier
Ne trespassa sans plor un tot seul jor entier,
U le main a lever u le soir a couchier
Ne ramembrast le duel de son droit eritier.

XXIX.
628 Quant ot Eufemïens le pelerin parler,
Por l'amor Alexin son ostel demander,
Lor li fait de son fil le duel renoveler.
Molt souspire del cuer, si commenche a plorer,
632 Sa maisnie regarde k'entor lui voit ester,
Par amor doucement les prent a aparler:
»S'or en i avoit un qui vosist creanter
Que il cest paumier qui revient d'outre mer
636 Voroit tote sa vie et servir et garder
Que ja en nule rien nel feroit contrister,
Par icel Damredieu qui nos a a saver
Le serf afrankiroie, ne l'en estuet doter,
640 Et ferai de ma terre si hautement caser
Qu'en tote ma ma[i]snie n'aroi[t]plus rice per.«
Es vos avant venu un adroit baceler,
Preu et douc, de bon aire, mais nel vos sai nomer.
644 Quant il ot son segnor si hautement jurer,
Le don a receü, ne vet pas refuser
Del pelerin servir et coucier et lever
Et fera tot ichou que il vera rover.

---

618 l. a Romme ancores r.
620 al pelerin
621 Por amur
622 Adonc li r. d.
623 ne men d.
629 Par amur
630 fait la dolur d. s. f. renoveir
632 regarde regarde . . . li
633 len prist a apeleir
634 q. moi v. loeir
635 icestui p.
636 Voloit

637 nel voldrat c.
638 q. vos at a gardeir
639 De s. lo frankiroie
640 feroi
641 aurat
642 Eh v. venut avant
643 Piu et dulz et cortois m.
644 h. parleir
645 nel volt
646 culchie
647 faire . . . quil li voldrat r.

XXX.

648 Or est saint Alexins en la maison entrés
Dont il se fu par nuit et fuïs et enblés,
De s'espeuse la belle partis et desevrés.
Asés par fu or grans la soie humilités,
652 Esmervilier s'en puet tote crestïentés,
Comment il puet si estre en son cuer adurés,
Quant ses peres li riches qui tant en est irés   [130a]
Come puet estre en sa vie par lui reconfortés,
656 Ne nel puet recoinoistre nus siens amis privés.
A l'entrer de la sale droit devant les degrés,
La fu saint Alexins ses hostés delivrés.
Por çou fu li saint hons en cel liu hostelés
660 Que ne vet pas li sires que il soit oubliés;
Veöir le vet sovent comment il soit gardés,
De quel part que il vegne, qu'il li soit presentés.
Le sergant commanda cui il fu commandés
664 Que tant com il vivra ne dura ses aés,
Ne li soit le mangiers de sa table veés,
Se gart que bien li face totes ses volentés.

XXXI.

A Rome est li saint hons por Dieu fais amosniers,
668 En sa maison demaine dont il ert eritiers,
Mais ne l'i conoist peres ne mere ne molliers,
N'en tote sa maisnie sergans ne escuiers;
En son petit hostel le sert ses despensiers,
672 Les amosnes manjue com autres provendiers;
Molt li est a delit et juners et viliers,
Orer et nuit et jor, ce est tos ses desiers.
De ces autres sergans i a molt d'avrisiers,
676 Car l'aigue dont il levent les mains a chevaliers
Li getent sor le cief, ce est grans destorbiers.

---

649 Donc
650 sa spose
652 Et mervilier
655 Ne pot estre
657 droit desor
658 deviseiz
659 Por huec . . . teil liu
660 s. quil i s.
661 il iert g.
662 viengniet

663 c. kil li soit ordineiz
666 Ce g.
668 d. donc il est
672 La rezoit les almones c.
673 d. jeuneirs et v.
674 jor et nuit . . . s. mestiers
675 D. ses a. s. at il m.
676.1 Les hamas par commant al maistre
      botilhiers
677 c., icest granz d.

Cascun jor l'escarnisent et dient reproviers
Et tafurs d'outre mer et enuieus pamiers.
680   Mais tot cho c'om li fait sostient il volentiers,
Bien set en son corage que tos ses encombriers
Li fait faire dÿables li siens mortés gerriers,
Mais s'il trek'en la fin parvint tés sodoiers,
684   En paradys celeste en iert grans ses leuwiers.

XXXII.

En itel penitanche et en tel noreture
Estuit saint Alexins par sa bone aventure
En la maison son pere en si grant covreture
688   Autres dis et set ans, si com dist l'escripture,
C'ainc ne pot reconoistre li viex s'engenreüre,
Ne sa mere Aglaël qui en fist sa porture.
Sovent pleurent por lui, molt est lor vie dure,
Ains puis qu'il le perdirent ne fu tenu mesure.   [130b]
Onkes tant ne li fisent si serjant de rancune
Que il lor respondist parole ne rancune.
Or aproisme li termes que sa vie la pure
696   Recevra sa merite et la cars sa droiture,
L'arme avra paradys et li cors sepulture.

XXXIII.

Quant voit saint Alexins que pres est de sa fin,
De paradys celeste est entrés el cemin,
700   Son despensier apele qui le sert soir et matin,
Si li fait enche quere et penne et parchemin.
Puis a tote sa vie escripte en latin,
Com le nori ses peres jovenchiel et meskin
704   Et il li quist mollier des filles Constentin,
Et com il s'en fuï fors del regne a tapin

---

678 reprochiers
678.1 Sovent i est por eaz apelez pauteniers
680 M. cant ke lom
681 B. s. enz en s. cuer ke t. ces e.
683 sil juska l. f. parmaint t.
684 li lowiers
685 paciensce
687 en ital c.
690 m. Glael ke fust sa p.
692 Quainc . . . nen f.
693 Nonkes . . . soi s.
694 ne laidure
695 aprochet li jors
696 son m., la c.
697 O om
700 q. sert s.
701 Et fait li q. penne e. enche e. p.
702 Tate s. v. escrist en son propre l.
703 s. jovenecel et m.
705 de Romme a t.

Et ala par la terre a loi de pelerin,
Et com fu a Rohais el regne barbarin
708 Et reçuit les amosnes a la gent de son lin;
En la maison son pere, le riche palasin,
Estuit dis et set ans c'ainc ne gosta de vin,
Ne ne se fist conoistre n'a parent n'a cousin,
712 N'a mere n'a mollier, n'a viellart n'a mescin.

XXXIV.

Quant ot saint Alexins sa parole finee
Et sa vie la bone escripte et recordee,
En sa main tint la cartre enclose et enseree,
716 Ja tant com il soit vis n'iert a home mostree.
De juner, de vilier en enstragne contree,
Descaus piés et en lagnes mainte terre passee,
Ne vet pas que tos jors soit sa bontés celee.
720 Par un saint dÿemenche quant la messe ert cantee
Et del peule de Rome estoit grans l'asamblee,
Ens el mostier saint Piere qui siet en la valee
Tot droit devant l'autel u elle ert consecree
724 Est une vois del ciel oïe et resonee
Dont la cités de Rome est trestote esfraee.

708-709
   Et receut les almones a guise de frairin,
   Et cum parlat lymegene al sogrestain ermin,
   Et cum partit diluec senz nul seut de voisin
   Et repairat a Romme a la gent de son lin,
710 ni g.
712 na vielh ne a m.
713 A. sorison parfineie
715 et envolepee
716.1 Mais Deus per cui il at tante paine
    endureie
718 piez en sa haire tante t.
719 volt . . . fust sa
720 est
722 Al m. de s. P.
722.1 In mala vicana par deza a lentreie
723 T. d. desor lauteir u lon dist la secreie
725 fut t.

712 n viellart ne mescin

XXXV.

La vois escrie en haut: »Ne dormés, mais veliés,
Venés a moi tot cil qui vos cuers traviliés

728   Et qui de mon service avés les cuers carciés,
Car li vostre repos vos est aparilliés!«
Li peule quant l'entent, tant par fu esmaiés,   [c]
Que ainc n'i ot si fort qui remasist sor piés,

732   Desor le pavement s'est cascuns apoiés,
Et proient le fil Dieu qui fu crucefiiés
Qu'il lor doinst patïence et pardoinst lor pechiés.

XXXVI.

Ensi comme le peules estoit en grant freör,

736   Cascuns gisoit a terre a larmes et a plor
Et sovent apeloient par cuer nostre signor,
La vois lor respondi: »Ne soiés en paor,
Alés vos ent trestout, li grant et li menor,

740   Si querés le saint home, ne faites mais sejor,
Cui Diex en paradys donra corone et flor,
Et proiiés li trestuit piuement par amor
Qu'il prit por la cité a nostre redemptor,

744   Car cel josdi promier par sonc l'abe del jor
Rendra s'arme la belle es mains nostre creator.«

XXXVII.

Or s'en torne li peule, n'i vet plus atargier,
Par tote la cité vont les rues cercier,

748   K'en quatre jors entiers ne font autre mestier,
Tant i sont ententif et en tel desirier;
Nus n'i vet euvre faire ne boire ne mangier,
Et quant il dont nel truevent n'i a que corechier.

---

727 v. cars
730 f. emmaiez
731 Kil ni ot un tant f. q. r. en p.
732 p. est c. aplaisiez
734 d. penitance
735 Issi . . . teil f.
736 en l. e. en p.
737 O *om*
739 Teneiz v. eu manois, tot et grant et m.
740 h., que ni f. s.
741 donrait

749 desierier

742 par dolzur
743 vostre r.
744 Ka ceste foit promiere p. sun
745 son c.
746 volt giens a.
746.1 De cel saint homme querre soi prist
      a travilhier
747 cite la citeit v. l. cercieir
748 Ke q. j. toz plains n.
749 T. i par s. entent . . . deseir
750 volt
751 donc

46

752 A josdi a matin revi[n]rent a mostier,
   Devant l'autel saint Piere se vont agenollier,
   Desor le pavement vont le marbre ba[i]sier,
   A larmes et a plor commenchent Dieu proier
756 Qu'il lor laist le saint home conoistre et cointier.
   La vois lor respondi: »Ne vos caut d'esmaiier,
   Eufemïens le garde qui l'a fait herbrigier,
   En sa maison demaine par un sien despensier.«

XXXVIII.

760 Quant oient li Romain la vois ensi parler,
   Del mostier a issir se prendent a haster,
   Devant l'empereör le vont araisoner,
   Doucement par amor, nel vellent aïrer.
764 »Sire, molt grant mervelle poons en toi viser;
   Por coi nos as tant fait travillier et pener
   Del home Dieu a quere par quatre jors laser?
   Et tu le nos as fait en ta maison celer!
   Comment le peuis tu en ton cuer endurer   [d]
   Que tu nel nos fesis le promier jor mostrer?
   Maine nos i, biax sire, si nos i fai parler;
   Si li proirons por Dieu de nos armes saver,
772 Et qu'il nos fache a Dieu nos pechiés pardoner.«
   Eufemïens l'entent si prist a souspirer,
   Si grant mervelle en ot tot le font trespenser.
   Il en jure de Dieu quank'il en puet penser
776 Qu'il onkes ne l'i sout ne ne l'oï nomer,
   Mais s'il l'i vellent quere, ne lor quier[t] a celer,
   Diex lor doinst par sa grase qu'il l'i pu[i]sent trover.

XXXIX.

   Quant oient la parole li doi empereör,
780 Archadys et Honeres, qui tenoient l'onor

752 par matin repairent al m.
754 p. et la terre b.
755 Ot l. e. ot p. pristrent D. a p.
756 h. troveir et acointier
757 L. v. li . . . c. emmaier
760 issi p.
761.1 Eufemien vunt querre la u virent esteir
763 vulent contrister
764 mut mervelle

752 a matin r. a matin mostier

768 C. tu lo poois en
769 fesisses al p. m.
770 Meneir
771 proierons tuit de
772 f. Deu
774 Iteil m. . . . len f.
775 Il lor j. . . . en seit p.
777 n. l. at a veeir
778 D. lo d. p. s. g. ke lom li puist t.

De l'empire de Rome en glorie a icel jor,
Eufemïen commandent doucement par amor
K'il voist a son hostel, si se meche en labor
784 De cel saint home quere dont il sont en error;
Et il iront aprés, la n'i feront sejor,
Si li vellent proiier por iaus et por les lor.

XL.

Vai s'ent Eufemïens tost et isnelement
788 Tot droit vers son palais u li peules l'atent;
Sa maisnie commande tost et isnelement
Sa sale aparillier de maint riche aornement,
De bons pailes grigois, de dosaus d'orïent.
792 Si serjant quant l'entendent ne s'atargent noient,
Ces bons tapis enstendent parmi le pavement,
Les samis et les pailes, les cendaus hautement,
La porte ont coronee et d'or kuit et d'argent,
796 De cases et de crois font grant aprestement.
Eufemïens meïsmes se paine durement
D'aparillier sa sale et sa cambre molt gent,
Ces encensiers enbrase et ces cierges esprent,
800 Car les empereörs a cui li mons apent
Et le saint apostoile c'om apele Inocent
Vet recevoir ensamble molt honerablement.
Son senescal apele qui despent son agent,
804 Belement li enquiert par amor doucement,
Par cele foit qu'il [doit] a Dieu omnipotent,   [131a]
De cel saint home Dieu s'il set a escïent
Qu'il soit en sa maison, si li die a present.
808 Et cil en jure Dieu par molt grant sacrement

---

781 glore
782 p. dulzor
783 Quil alht . . . s. soi mete e.
784 D. querre lo s. h. par cui s. e. freor
785 a. quil n.
786 Quar lui v.
786.1 Kil lur proiet mercit a Deu lo creator
788 lo palais
790 ditant r.
791 grezois
792 O om

804 enquierent   807 as prement

794 O om
796 D. c. de croiz
797 O om
798 O om
799 Ses e. . . . ses c.
801 cui lom clainme I.
802 Voldrat en sa maison rezoivre haltement
803 despensoit sa gent
806 D. si s.
807 soit soit . . ., quil d.
808 len . . . m. halt s.

C'ainc n'en oï novelle ne il n'en set noient.
Quant l'ot Eufemïens, si sospire forment,
Molt par fu esmaiés et le cuer ot dolent,
812 Quant il de cel saint home nen ot asentement;
Les iex dreça al ciel vers Dieu omnipotent,
Molt sospire del cuer et pleure tenrement
Et proie Damredieu del cuer parfondement
816 Que del saint cors li fache acun demostrement.
Mais ne li targera des or mais longement;
Il le vera as iex par tel atornement
Et la mere al saint home et s'espeuse ensement.

XLI.
820 Dementrueus que li viex estoit en tel penser
De cel saint home quere que il ne puet trover,
Estes vos les serjant qui le sieut ministrer
Vers son signor s'aproisme la u le vit ester.
824 »Eufemïen, biax sire, por Dieu, car fai garder
De cel saint home Dieu dont je t'oï demander,
Que ce ne soit ichis que m'as fais ministrer
Hui a dis et set ans, car je l'ai fait conter
828 C'adés li ai aidié a coucier, a lever.
Onkes de tos les homes dont ai oï parler
N'oï d'un qui peuist tant vilier ne juner;
Onques ne vi sa bouce ne nuit ne jor cesser
832 De loenges Dieu dire ne de satiers canter,
N'onkes tant ne le vi ta maisnie gaber
Ne clamer patonier ne tafur d'outre mer
C'ainc le veïse point le corage muer.
836 Sovent vi tes sergans, mais nel poc amender,
Que li faisoient l'aigue sor la teste verser

---

809 il en s.
810 E. cant lot, mut s.
811-814 O om
815 p. a D.
817 t. mie mut l.
818 Kil lo v. alz p. t. acointement
819 Quil en aurat lo cuer correzos
et dolant
821 saint h. a qurre quil n. pooit t.
822 Eh v. l. menestreit q. l. suet despenser
823 saprochet l. u il l. v. steir

824 c. engardeir
825 Dicel sait . . . toi contristeir
826 icil q. tu . . . f. gardeir
827 car bien lai f.
828 aidiet et c. et l.
830 ne oreir
831 ne jur ne nuit c.
832 spalmes
835 len veisse jor lo c.
836 pou
837 Kil li . . . t. jeteir

812 ont   828 a o coucier

Et feroient el cief por lui a destorber.
Nus hons char sans lui nel peüst endurer,
840 La soie humilité ne puet nus hons esmer.
Encor i a tot el que je vos vel conter:
Ier matin par sonc l'abe quant il dut ajorner,
Me fist parchemin quere et enche demander, [b]
844 En sa main tint la cartre ne le vet pas mostrer,
Ains ne le peuc veöir tant me seüisse pener
Se tu ne m'en ves croire, sempres le pues prover.«

XLII.
Quant ot Eufemïens et entent la vreté
848 Del saint home dont cil li a dit et contét,
Isnelement s'atorne, n'i a plus demorét;
La u il set son hoste de desous le degré
Devant le lit s'areste et si l'a apelé
852 Doucement par amor, mais il n'a mot sonét.
Son bel cief li descuevre, sel treve devïé,
Mais la chiere de lui li rent si grant clarté
Com soit angles del ciel u solaus en esté.
856 Lor s'aperçoit li sires et set en seürté
Que c'estoit li saint hons dont la vois dut parler,
De pitié et de joie en a des iex ploré,
Vers orïent se couche, s'en a Dieu aeuré,
860 En plorant en merchie la haute trinité.
Li briés c'out en sa main estoit envolepés,
Vot reçoivre a saint home, mais nen ot poësté,
Et quant ne le puet traire a Dieu l'a commandé;
864 El palais se repaire tot de marbre listé,
Vint as empereörs, si lor a devisé

---

838 col
839 de char
840 p. nuz aesmeir
841 q. v. v. reconteir
842 diet
843.1 Si escrist tote jor fresci ka lenvespreir
844 tient
845 Ainc n. la pou avoir t. ne men sou p.
846 Et s. t. nel vuls croie
849–850
    Isnelement sen vait la u son osteil seit
852 mais cil

854 lor r.
855 Ke s.
856 sot a segurteit
857 Ke zastoit . . . v. ot p.
858 et damur en ot d.
859 Turnat v. o. sen
860 O om
861 la main estroit e.
863 nel en pot t.
864 Al p. en r. t. lo m. listreit
865 desviseit

50

Que Diex li a as iex le saint home mostré
Par son serjant demaine qui main[t] jor l'a gardé,
868 Qui li porte tiesmoign et los de grant bonté,
Dis et set ans l'a bien com saint home prové.
Le consel a sergant lor a dit et conté,
Le splendor de sa face et la grant dignité
872 Que en lui a veüs, mais que mort l'a trové.
Inocens, l'apostoiles, et vesque et abé,
Par les degrés de marbres en sont jus avalé,
Eufemïens les gui[e] droit desous les degré.
876 Quant vinrent al saint home cors, si l'ont si bel trové
Comme estoile de mer u angle coroné;
Or en iert tot ichou, ja nen iert trestorné
Que Diex en a el ciel devant lui ordené.

XLIII.
880 Li doi empereör o le pape Inocent
Estont devant le cors en piés el pavement,   [c]
En grant humilité enclin et passïent.
Archadys, l'empere, parla promierement,
884 Devant le cors se couche, si pleure tenrement.
»Biax sire, ne despire selonc ton ensïent
La nostre humle proiere por Dieu omnipotent.
Nos somes pecheör ensi com autre gent,
888 Porquant somes nos cil as qués li mons apent,
Et a cest apoistoile a cui li mons s'atent,
Car sainte glise garde et d'infer le desfent.
Lasque, sire, ta main, por Dieu commandement,
892 Si nos baille le chartre, d'amor le nos consent
Veöir que dedens a, por ton commandement!«

---

866 Cum D.
867 q. tanz ans
868 Kil l. . . . de sa b.
869 Lat par d.
870 lor a tot reveleit
871 La s. d. la chiere et
872.1 Li empereor loent, del banc sunt
     sus leveit
874 O om
875 g. de desor l.
876 virent lo s. c.
877 e. del ciel

879 en c.
883 parlat parlat p.
884 O om
885 despitier
887 Se n. s. p. aussi c.
888 P. huec si summes c. a cui lempire a.
889 trestoz l. m. sasent
890 nos defent
891 Lascier
892 bailier l. c. et dammur n.
893 par Deu c.

866 as cex   877 a u   884 pleeure   887 pe somes

XLIV.

Inocens, l'apostoiles, ot le cors segurtain,
Si s'aproisme al saint cors qu'il vit de grase plain,
896   Ses mains tent a la cartre, il li lasque la main;
Quant il l'ot receüe et traite de sa main,
Si le rendi avant a un sien capelain,
A maistre cancelier qui n'ot pas le cuer vain;
900   Essïo ot a non, s'ot le cuer large et sain,
Cil le list en oiant tot le peule romain.
Ja oront tel mervelle et itant douc reclain
Dont tot seront en plor, et cortois et vilain.

XLV.

904   Essïo list la cartre qui bien en fu apris,
Et on [li] fist tel pais que nus hons qui fust vis
N'osa un mot soner, ne jovene ne antis.
A tos fait connisanche que c'est saint Alexis,
908   Li fix Eufemïen qui en la biere est mis,
Qui s'en fuï de Rome, hui a pasé maint dis,
Et degerpi s'onor, son pere et son païs
Por l'amor Jhesu Crist, le roi de paradys.
912   Eufemïens l'entent, tel dolors l'a conquis,
Pasmés caï a terre desor le marbre bis,
Ausi tainst comme cendre et enpali le vis.
Et quant il se redrece, si se claime caitis,
916   Dolens, maleüreus, seus et povres d'amis,
A ambes mains detrait sa barbe o le poil gris,
Trestot son vestement a desront et malmis,
Or voroit estre mors, poise lui qu'il est vis.

---

895 Il saprochet a. c. cui v.   909 at eut m.
896 S. doiz . . . lasche   910 sa femme e.
897 son sain   911 P. amur J. C., cavoir volt p.
898 Puis   912 ait
899 q. non ot l.   913 mabre
900 c. saive e.   914 Issi t. c. c. e. paleist el v.
902 Sempre o.   915 Cant . . . redrezoit
905 lom . . . nes h. ni gronis   917 p. bis
906 O om   918 derrot
907 f. conissant ke ce ert A.   919 li

915 se ch claime   916 maleuvireus   917 pols

52

XLVI.

Ainçois qu'Eufemïens euist la cartre oïe,   [d]
Ne remasist en piés por tot l'or de Rosie,
Sa teste la cenue et sa barbe florie
Desront a ambes mains et son cors martir[i]e
924   Si com hons forsenés a la presse partie
Et fiert ses puens ensamble que fait grant retentie.
Ensement se depane comme cose esmarie
Et maine tant grant duel por poi ne pert la vie;
928   Devers le cors s'aproisme qui forment resplendie,
Deseure s'est pasmés, s'a la biere saisie,
A ambes mains l'enbrache, ne le vet laisier mie.
Quant li cuers li revint dont pleure et brait et crie:
932   »E Alexin, biax fix, com dure departie!
Por coi as fait a ton pere itant grant felonie,
Comment le peut souffrir la toie compagnie
De tant jor c'as esté en la nostre balie,
936   C'ainc ne nos confortas tant com dura ta vie?
Or deuissiés, biax fix, govrener ta maisnie,
Ton pere conforter, ta mere l'esmarie,
Et t'espeuse la belle qui toi pas nen oublie;
940   Mais ce nen iert ja mais, car ta mors est fenie.
Las! n'i a mais atente, m'esperance est falie.«

XLVII.

»Biax fix,« ce dist li peres, »u prendrai mais confort?
Del grant duel u je sui ne venrai mais a port,
944   Quant a mes iex te voi devant moi gisir mort.
Je cuidoie, biax fix, mais perdu ai mon sort,
K'encor deuisse avoir de toi joie et deport;
Mais ce nen iert ja mais, n'i atent nus resort.
948   Diex, por coi vi ge tant? Certes, çou est a tort.«

---

920 Azois . . . por ait l.
924 O *om*
925 Si f. . . . e. ken f.
926 Altressi soi d.
927 O *om*
928 O *om*
929 Desor lo cors soi pahmet, . . .
    b. embracie
930 O *om*
931 si p., b. et c.
933 P. kas f. . . . iss g.

934 Deus, cum lo pot s.
935 t. ans
936 ne men c.
937 chastuer t.
939 ta spose
940 mors men defie
941 ni ai
942-943
    Del grant peril u sui ne venrai mais a **port**,
    Beaz fiz, ce dist, u penrai mais confort?
948 Certes, mut ai grant t.

XLVIII.

»Encore avoie, fix, en mon cuer esperance
Que tu a acun jor aprés longe atendanche
Deuisses repairier, par fine ramenbranche
952   De la dolor ton pere cui laisses en erranche
Et moi reconforter et tolir ma pensanche
Et mon cors enfoïr, si com ert ma fïanche,
Et m'ounor maintenir a force et a poisanche,
956   Mais or en sui del tot caüs en desperanche
Diex, u prendrai mais confort ne aliganche,
Quant jesir voi en biere de celui la sanblance,
Por cui i ai esté tant an en esfraanche.   [132a]
960   Et tot le mont cercié sans nule aseguranche?
Et Mors, por coi te targes, por coi fais demorance,
Plus te desire m'arme que dou mont l'onoranche,
Or voroie estre mors sans nule repentanche!«
964   Molt a el cuer li peres grant duel et grant pesanche,
Mais quant le seut la mere qui le nori d'enfanche,
De la dolor de li ne sai faire esmanche.

XLIX.

Dementrues que li peres a la teste meslee
968   Ensi pleure et gaimente dolor renovelee,
Es vos tos les degrés sa mere l'esgaree
La novelle a oïe qui pas ne li agree;
Ensi desront la presse et maine tel crïee
972   Comme beste savage qui soit descainee.
De tote sa vesture a a ses mains depanee,
Sanglante sa maiselle, tote est descevelee,
Et ensi crie et brait comme riens forseenee,
976   Que sa grant honesté a trestote oubliee.
Elle crie a la gent k'est illuec asanblee:
»E! car me faites voie, bone gens honoree!«
Si vera la caitive sa dure destinee,

---

951 p. droite r.   965 q. lot n.
952 laissas   968 Issi . . . sa d. renoveie
954 c. sepelir   969 Eh v.
957 ja mais   971 Issi d.
959 P. c. ai por t. a. esteit en e. 973 Tote s. v. a. ses m.
961 Ei M., . . . tatarges   974 ses mammeles, t. d.
963 Mon vulh seroie m.   975 Issi c. e. braut c.
964 O om   978 Ei

980 La dolereuse portee dont ja n'iert confortee.
Quant elle vint a cors, deseure s'est pasmee,
Tainte est si comme cendre et roide et abosmee,
Ensi l'a sa dolors et conquise et menee
984 Que li aquant cuidierent que a fin fust alee.
Quant elle se redreche, elle fu respiree,
Si fiert ses puens ensamble, a poi ne s'est tuee;
A haute vois escrie comme feme dervee:
988 »E Alexin, biax fix, com m'avés contristee
De la vostre sanblanche que tant m'avés celee,
Ja tant ne vivrai mais que ne soie esploree.
En la maison ton pere as esté a enblee
992 Que un povres pamiers qui fust d'autre contree.
Sire en deuissiés estre! E Diex, quele ostelee,
Fix, nos t'i avons fait en ta vie privee!
O si comme a un povre t'ert despense donee,
996 Entre nos est ta vie povrement definee.
Por toi n'arai mais joie, tote en sui desperee;
Or deuisses, biax fix, maintenir t'espousee,   [132b]
Ton pere conforter, ta mere l'esgaree,
1000 Et govrener deuisses ta maisnie privee.
Mais ce nen iert ja mais, or est ma joie alee
Et tote m'atendance est hui cest jor finee;
Or voroie estre morte sans nule demoree.
1004 E Mos, car me prenés, com seroie buer nee
Se je ere o mon fil pres de lui enseree!«

L.
»Biax fix,« ce dist la mere, »com ai fait longe atente,
Tans ans que m'as veü por toi triste et dolente
1008 En la maison ton pere qui por toi se gaimente.
Viax quant nos t'apieliemes, jo et t'espeuse gente,
Por coi ne nos disoies de toi aucun asente?

---

980 perde
981 si sest desor p.
982 T. comme la c.
983 Issi lat la d. e. c. e. mueie
984 q. fust a fin a.
985 quele f.
987 O om
988 Ei
989 v. presence qui t. nos ert c.

990-1005
        Por toi naurai mais joie,
        del tot sui despereie (997)
1007 T. a. cum m.
1008 pere u ge toi represente
1008.1 Cant ne nos confortas? Mut eus
        dure entente (1015)
1009-1010 O om

Trop par euis dur cuer, ne sai que je t'en mente.

1012 Diex, com le pot souffrir nus hons de ta jovente,
Quant veöies ton pere et ta mere plorente
Et t'espeuse la belle qui por toi se demente,
C'ainc ne nos confortas? Molt euis dure entente.

1016 Isi grant cruaté ja mais Diex ne consente;
Se vivoie cent ans, vin u quarante u trente
Ne sera mais uns jors que la dolor ne sente,
Car ice me confont et ocist et tormente

1020 Que tos jors t'ai doné et vie et vestemente
Com a autre paumier qui por Dieu se presente,
K'ainc ne poc porveöir que fuise ta parente.
Diex! ja morai de duel et li cuers me gaimente,

1024 Quant ne me reconforte qui sor tos m'atalente.«

LI.

»E fix,« ce dist la mere, »comment le puis sofrir
Que cascun jor veöies tant plor et tant sospir
De ton pere et de moi qui t'aviens nourit?

1028 A tes sergans demaine te laisoies laidier
Et dire les reproches et sor ton cief ferir;
Molt par ert fors li cuers qui le pooit soufrir,
Quant tu ne le pooies a ton pere jehir.

1032 Et Diex, por coi faisoies si mon cuer esmarir
Et mon cuer aveuler que ainc ne peuc coisir
Que ce fust Alexis, mes fix, dont voi marir?
Iceste racordanche ne me puet mais falir,

1036 Cis Diex ne me laira treske devrai morir.«
Tant fort baise le cors u ke le puet sentir,   [c]
La ciere angelial que tant voit resplendir,
Et enbrache le cors la u le voit gesir,

1011-1012 O om
1013 m. dolente
1014 ta spose . . . soi gaimente
1016 n. confente
1020 tant j.
1021 a. frairin
1022 n. pou parcivoir
1023 me cravente
1024 Cant cil ne moi conforte q.
1025 Ei . . . cum l. poois s.
1027 norrir

1028 Et t. . . . laidir
1029 lor
1030 quil p. sortenir
1031 ne toi volois a ton p.
1032 p. ke sofroies s. m. sens e.
1033 avogleir cant nel pooi chiesir
1034 d. tant mair
1035 p. pas f.
1036 Dolerose de toi troske moi fras m.
1038 angelical
1039 e. la biere

1020 vestemenche   1029 les les proeces   1031 tor pere

1040	A poi que ne se tue c'om ne le puet tenir.
	Molt fait grant duel la mere por Alexis son fil,
	A haute vois escrie c'om le puet bien oïr:
	»Ahi! tot nostre ami qui nos devés servir
1044	De mon fil conforter, castoyer et blandir,
	Estoit vostre esperanche qu'il deuist revenir.
	A mes iex le voi, lase, mais ne me vet oïr,
	Ne parler a sa mere, conforter ne joïr;
1048	Car plorés, totes gens, qui nos veés perir
	Et a si grant dolor nostre honor revertir!
	Quant je mon fil voi mort, n'ai soing de moi garir,
	Tote sui desperee, ne sai mais u fuïr,
1052	Ja mais n'istrai de duel dusc'al jor del fenir.«

LII.

	Es vos parmi la place la pucelle acorant,
	Qu'ert espeuse al saint home et atendut l'ot tant,
	Vestue de noirs dras qui bien sont conisant
1056	La veveté de lui et le dolor pensant.
	Quant elle vint a lui u le cors vit gisant,
	Deseure s'est pasmee et la biere embraçant;
	Quant vint de pasmisons, se fait un duel si grant,
1060	A ses mains le rembrace a hate vois criant,
	A poi que n'est estainte sor le cors en baisant.
	Molt fort pleure et brait et ses mains detordant,
	Et maine tel dolor, ne soit hons qui demant
1064	C'ainc mais ne fist tel peine ne mere son enfant.

LIII.

| | »Sire,« ce dist s'espeuse, »com or sui desperee! |
| | Molt ai fait longe atente et dure desiree, |

1040 n. len puet partir
1041 O *om*
1042 O *om*
1043 Ohi! . . . n. soliez s.
1044 chastuer e.
1045 Zastoit
1049 En si g. desperance la n. h. vertir
1052 Toz jors serai em plor troskal tens
     de morir
1053 Eh v. p. l. presse
1054 et ratendut lat t.
1055 b. funt c.
1064 t. feine

1056 vevee
1057 v. illuec . . . voit g.
1058 O *om*
1059–1060
     A ambes mains lembracet et fait
     un dol si grant
1061 p. nen est e.
1062 Ot mut halt plor sescrie et s.
1063 quil d.
1064 Kainc ne f. m. iteil ne mere de senfant
1065 sa spose
1066 d. desevreie

Dolente moi caitive et veve et esgaree,
1068 Je cuidoi[e] encore estre aucun jor confortee.
Mais ce nen iert ja mais, tel est ma destinee,
Quant cis ne me conforte cui je sui esposee,
De cui je deuisse estre a tors jors honoree.
1072 Or puis mais bien dire que ma joie est alee,
Car ne serai ja mais de ses iex esgardee,
Ne ne sera ma bouche a la soie privee.
Hui est ma grans dolors en mon cors renovelee   [d]
1076 Qui en tote ma vie ne sera desevree.«

LIV.

»Amis,« ce dist s'espeuse, »or sui venue a jor
Que trestote ma joie est mue en tristor.
A loi de toterele qui eskive verdor,
1080 Deduirai mais mon cors et vivrai en labor,
N'escouterai mais cant ne ne porterai flor,
Ne desir mais del siecle le joie ne l'onor.
A tos jors arai mais vest[e]üre de plor,
1084 Tors jors serai mais veve, n'ai soing d'atre signor.«
Tant fort ploroit li peules qui veöit la dolor
Com cil font sor le cors qui l'aiment par tenror,
N'i veïssiés sans larmes un seul, grant ne menor.

LV.

1088 Inocens, l'apostoiles, quant çou ot escouté,
Et li empereör qui molt l'ont esgardé,
En un vasel molt gent et molt bien aorné
Ont le cors a saint home honestement posé.

1069 jor mais, t. irt m.
1070 j. fui e.
1072 ja mais
1073 jor mais . . . engardeie
1075 la g. . . . renoveie
1076 defineie
1077 A., or est la triste venue a icel jor
1078 ma vie iert turneie en t.
1079.1 Qui naurat mais pareil cant pert
sa prime amur

1072 puise   1087 .I. g seul

1080 m. ma vie et v. a l.
1081.1 Ne ne vestirai purpre ne drap
ditei colur
1082 m. la glore del s.
1083.1 Ja daltre companie ne moi doinst
Deus valur
1086 Ke cil
1088 cant ot tot e.

58

1092	De riches dras de soie l'ont bien envolepé,
	Sor la biere le lievent par molt grant honesté,
	Un blanc samit a or ont par desous geté.
	A lor cors le leverent li plus rice barné,
1096	En la place l'en porterent droit enmi la cité;
	Puis font [noncier] a peule et dire par vreté
	Que il ont le saint home le digne cors trové.
	Quant oient la parole cil qui sont tant pené
1100	De quere le saint home travilié et pené,
	Lor mains tendent a ciel, si ont Dieu mercïë.
	Tot le keurent veöir, car molt l'ont desiré;
	Tant i akeurent gent de par la grant cité
1104	Que molt fu grans la presse quant furent asamblé.
	Nus hons n'aproisme a cors de si grant enferté
	Que par main ne l'ait Diex et gari et sané.
	Assés i ot le jor aveules ralumés
1108	Et contrait redrechié, y trope desenflé;
	Li sourt i ont oï et li muel parlé,
	De maint cors d'ome i sont li dÿable jeté,
	Tote ont le jor perdue illuec lor poësté.
1112	Quant le saint apostoiles connut la dignité,
	Haradis et Honeres, li doi roi coroné, [133a]
	Del saint home dont Diex a le mont alumé,
	De pitié et de joie en ont des iex ploré,
1116	Lors mains tendent a ciel, si ont Dieu mercïë
	Des mervelles qu'il voient et hautement loé
	Et grant grase rendues et parfont encliné.

LVI.

| | Quant voit li apostoiles les malades saner |
| 1120 | Et li empereör qui Rome ont a garder |

1092-1095:
    Dun blanc samit a or estroit envolepeit,
    Sor la biere lo lievent par mut grant honesteit
1096 portent d. parmi l.
1098 s. cors del saint homme t.
1099 qui tant sunt p.
1100 h. et vencut et lasseit
1101 O *om*
1103 O *om*
1104 Mut par fut g. l. p. cant il sont a.
1105 naprochet

1106 Caparmain n.
1107 i sunt
1108 redreciet et droppe d.
1110 c. i s. dommes li d.
1111 l. posteeit
1113 Archadis et Honorís
1115 et damur
1116 O *om*
1117 v. ont Dammrideu l.
1118 p. adoreit
1119 Q. la. v.

1094 blant   1106 garir   1108 redrechier   1111 le e jor   1113 et et

Contrais salir de joie, aveules ralumer
Et les ardans destaindre, ydrope desenfler
Por le merite al saint, et les muiaus parler,
1124 Dieu commencent de joie hautement a loer.
A lor [cols] le leverent, sel prisent a porter
Par grant humilité et por lui honorer,
Et qu'il lor face a Dieu lor pechiés pardoner;
1128 Mais tant est grans la presse, nus hons n'i puet aler.
Qui la veïst la gent de partot asanler,
Acorir par ces rues et a cors arester
Et la biere baisier qui tant i puet presser
1132 Qu'il i puist aprochier ne ses mains adeser,
La peuist on mervelles de ses iex regarder.
Li empereör voient le grant peule asanler
Et a la gent menue si grant presse mener,
1136 Lor tresoriers commandent deniers a aporter
Et argent et monoies et besans d'outre mer;
Par les rues les font aprés lor dos jeter,
Par les deniers se cuident del peule delivrer,
1140 Mais nïent ne lor vaut quank'il i font j[e]ter,
Car por l'avoir ne vellent povre gent retorner.

LVII.
Tant par fu grans la presse et li bruis de la gent
C'om lor fait par ces rues jeter or et argent
1144 Por la presse partir, mais ne lor vaut noient,
Que tant par sont trestuit vers le saint cors entent,
Ne presient deniers por tot l'or d'orïent.
Cil se tient molt a rice qui a ses mains le sent,
1148 Ne qui puet a sa bouce tocher son vestement.
A paine et a dolor, a mervillous torment,
Parvinrent a mostier la u li cuers lor tent,
Droit a saint Bonefache u gisent si parent   [b]

1122 O om
1123 P. la graze a. s. home et
1124 O om
1127 Por kes l. . . . p. pardeir
1129 v. lo pople d.
1130 Acurre
1132 puet a. ne a lui a.
1133 Del desier poust grant m. ensgardeir
1134 Quat le. v. si g. p. ajosteir
1136 Son t. . . . apresteir
1138 P. la rue lur fait derrier lor
1139 P. ce soi quide issi del
1140-1141
        Mais riens ne li esploite, nuz ni vult
        returner
1142 Mult p.
1143 Om . . . c. places espandre o.
1145 Car t. . . . v. l. c. si e.
1146 N. proisset nule rien trestot lo.
1147 sa main
1149 A m. traval, a p. et a t.
1151 Del cors s. B.

1152   Le voront enfoïr se Diex lor consent.

LVIII.

Quant ont posé le cors del saint home el mostier,
A grant paine font traire le peule un poi arier,
Les clers aler avant et al cors aproismier.
1156   Li apostoiles fait l'obseque commencier;
Quant l'entendent li clerc ne se font proier,
Cantent ymnes, leçons, por Dieu a grasiier
Vers et respons et preces et trestot lor satier
1160   Que en set jors tos plains ne font autre mestier.
La veïsiés le peule en molt grant desirier
Devant le cors orer et la biere baisier,
Ces dras terdre a lor iex qui s'en puet asier!
1164   Or a cascuns laisor qu'il s'en puet aaisier
As malades saner, as contrais redrecier.
Un sepulcre molt riche fisent aparillier
Li doi empereör et molt bien entaillier
1168   De pieres precieuses et d'or kuit favrechier
Et tot d'evre grigoise souticement entaillier;
Puis si fisent le cors al saint home couchier.
La veïsiés le jor serviche molt plenier,
1172   Tant candelabre d'or et tant bon encensier,
Tantes crois d'or et casses qui molt font a proisier,
On n'i vet pas l'encens ne le mirre espargnier,
Le jor en i ot ars assés plus d'un sestier.

LIX.

1176   Quant orent le saint cors el sepulcre posé,
De riches dras de soie bellement aorné,
De grans bendias d'orfrois honestement bendé,

1152 valdront sevelir s. D. le lor c.
1155 aprochier
1156 Les exekes commande li pape a c.
1157 O *om*
1158 C. psalmes, l.
1159 V. e. lezons . . . lo psaltier
1161 Donc v. l. p. a m. g. deseier
1163 Ses d. t. a ses olz
1164 lascor . . . p. satiier
1164.1 Asseiz i at grant gent casche
     mut al guaitier
1171 Le

1164.2 La li mostrat bien Deus quil
     lavoit forment chier
1168 De precioses p. . . . favrigier
1169 subtilment entalhir
1170 Puis i f. l. c. del s.
1173 T. croiz et chasses dor q.
1174 Lom ni volt p.
1175 ont
1178 g. nales

Et le sepulcre clos et par tot bien seré,
1180 Ne s'en erent encore li Romain retorné;
Dont lor saut une odors de si grant dignité,
C'onques n'ot telle espese ne nule flors de pré,
Ne nule herbe del mont dont on ait poësté;
1184 Ainc n'ot si bone odor en la crestïenté,
Car il i sont le jor malade maint sané.

LX.

Quant voient li Romain le don al creator
Qui tant lor fait de bien et de joie et d'onor,
1188 Car paradys lor euvre et lait sentir l'odor,
Et sane les malades et jete de languor,   [c]
Les aveules ralume, les contrais rent valor
Por le merite al saint qui conquise a s'amor,
1192 Tuit en rendent merchi et grase al redemptor
Et aeurent de cuer Jhesum lor redemptor
Qui si lor a muee en joie lor tristor.
Or proions Damredieu le nostre creator
1196 Que, s'il por nos pechiés a envers nos iror
Dont nos soions caü es mains a souduitor,
Que il par la proiiere a cest bon confessor
Nos maint a sa lumiere et ost de tenebror,
1200 Vers nos demete s'ire et nos rende s'amor.
Signor, de ce saint home faisons nos mireör!
Oï avés sa vie com vesqui sans error,
Bien gerpi de cest siecle et la joie et l'onor;
1204 Povres i fu por Dieu, n'i ot cure d'onor,
Par bien faire a aquis la grant joie angelor.
Prenons a lui exemple, se serons molt millor,
Ensi serons delivres del mal engigneör,
1208 Si en irons a Dieu tot sans nule paor.
Signor, contre dÿable soions fort en estor,
Proions saint Alexin tot a une clamor
Et tos les saint del ciel (molt), qui en grant resplendor

1179 b. saeleir
1180 R. tot turneit
1181 Lors lor
1182 Konkes nule e. ne n. f. desteit
1183 N. n. riens en m. d. lom a. posteeit
1184 O *om*
1185 Par cel i s. l. j. maint malade s.

1186 la donne
1187 j. e. damur
1188 Ke p. . . . et fait s.
1191 c. at lonor
1193 del c. J. lo salveor
1194 Ki ssi lor at meneie
1195-1211 O *om*

1212	Vivent sans fin en joie avec lor creator,
	Que il proient por nos a Dieu nostre signor
	Qu'il nos doinst en cel siecle faire tel labor
	En juner, en orer, en larmes et en plor,
1216	Que, quant il nos venra jugier a derain jor,
	Et seront devant lui et juste [et] pecheör
	Et tranbleront li angle et avront grant paor
	Apostoile et martir, juges et confessor,
1220	Que nos soions si digne c'avoir puisons s'amor,
	Et que en paradys nos doinst corone et flor.
	Amen dites trestuit, li grant et li menor,
	Que Diex le nos otroit par la soie doçour!
1224	Or est dite la vie d'un glorieus signour.
	Amen!

1212-1224 O *om*

TABLE OF PROPER NAMES

Abagarons 336: King of Rohais, q.v.

Aglaël 133, 690: mother of Alexis and wife of Euphemian.

Alexin 167, 330, 1210, etc.: Alexis.

Archadys 780, 883: Arcadius, the Eastern Roman emperor (395-408), son of Theodosius I, the Great, and older brother of Honorius. See *Honeres*, below.

Babyloiene 417 (*Babylone-*), fem.: Babylon.

Boneface 153; Bonefache 1151 (*Bonifatiu-*), masc., Boniface I (Saint), 44th pope (418-422).

Caples 316 (*Claples* in Oxford MS.): Constantinople? (*Caples* may perhaps stand for *Cpolis*, the customary abbreviation employed for Constantinople. Cf. Codex Vallicensis collated by the Bollandists: "descendit autem Capolim, ascendensque navem."

Constentin 704: Constantine I, the Great, Roman emperor (306-337).

Damredieu 271, 286, 395, etc.; Damrediex 567 (vocative sing.), masc. noun, orthographic variant of *Damedieu, Damnedieu, Damledeu*, etc. (der. from *Dominu-*, + *Deu-*), Lord God.

David 50, 455: David, king of Israel (cir. 1010-975 B.C.).

Deu 19, 25, 35, etc.; Dieu 4, 9, 58, etc. (*Deu-*), masc. noun, God; nom. sing. *Dex* 48, 243; *Diex* 7, 45, 246, etc.

Elysabeth 53: Elizabeth (Saint), wife of Zachariah/Zachary, q.v., and mother of Saint John the Baptist.

Essio 900, 904: chancellor (=chief secretary) of Pope Innocent.

Eufemïen 34, 606, 782, etc. (*Euphemianu-*): father of Saint Alexis.

Haradis 1113 (See *Archadys*).

Honeres 780, 1113: Honorius (Flavius-Augustus), Roman emperor of the West (395-423). See Archadys.

Hrohais 328 (See *Rohais*).

Inocent 801, 873, 880, etc.: Innocent I (Saint and Confessor), 42nd pope (402-417).

Israël 50: Israel (Saint).

Jehan 285: Saint John the Evangelist.

Jhesu Crist 332, 911: Jesus Christ; vocative sing. *Jhesu Cris* 397, 467; *Jhesum* 1193 (obl. sing.).

Landise 320, 324; Landisse 579, 580: Laodicea, city of Syria, on the sea-coast (now Latikiah/Latakia or Ladikiveh/Ladikieh).

Marie 51, 519 (Low Latin Maria-): The Virgin Mary.

Piere 722, 753: Peter (Saint).

Pol 583: Paul (Saint).

Rohais 330, 364, 473: Edessa, city of Mesopotamia, in the province of Osrhoëne, now Rhoa or Orfa; the form Rohais appears for the city of Edessa in many medieval texts based on the Latin legend while the earlier 11th century version has *Alsis* (MS. L),

64

Arsis (MS. A), *Axis* (MS. P), *Aussi* (MS. S), and *Alis* (MS. M). All these forms go back
to the original Alsis, but just how *Edessus* became *Alsis* is difficult to ascertain[1].

Rome 10, 26, 117, etc. (*Roma-*), fem.: Rome.

Rosie 921: Rosia or Rosea, a very fertile district near Reate (now *le Roscie*).

Sarra 47; Sarram 455: Sarah, wife of Abraham and mother of Isaac.

Sire 381; Syre 318, 326 (Syria-), fem.: Syria.

Tarses 582: Tarsus, small city of Cilicia (ancient country and region on the coast of
SE Asia Minor), on the historic Cydnus river. Saint Alexis was attracted to Tarsus
(birthplace of Saint Paul, the apostle) by its famous sanctuary consecrated to
Saint Paul.

Tobïe 454: Tobias.

Zacharie 53: Zachariah/Zachary, jewish priest, husband of Saint Elizabeth and father of
Saint John the Baptist.

----

1 See Gaston Paris et L. Pannier. *La vie de St. Alexis* (Paris, 1872), p. 180.

GLOSSARY

Amesniers 404, Amosnier 172, 667: one who receives alms.

Anemi 568: enemy (=the Devil).

Anguoseus 201: much distressed, in anguish.

Apieliemes 1009: imperfect 4 of *apeler*.

Ardans 1122: those afflicted with convulsions, gangrene or psychic disorders. It should be mentioned that the "mal des ardents", an epidemic lasting from the 10th to the 12th cent., was characterized by the aforementioned physical and mental disorders.

Aveules 1107, 1121, 1190: (the) blind.

Aviens 1027: imperfect 4 of *avoir*.

Avrisiers 675: enemies.

Awan 308: more.

Belisor 129: more beautiful, noble.

Bendias 1178: bands, strips (of cloth).

Besans 1137: small gold coins.

Bis 913: of a dark brownish-grey.

Blandir 1044: to care for.

Buer 1004 (*bona hora*), adv.: in a good hour, auspiciously.

Casé 30: enfeoffed, id est, Euphemian was a nobleman (a liege lord) invested with a fief which had a habitation and he had 300 liege men bound to give him allegiance and service.

Cases 796; Casses 1173: reliquaries (small boxes, caskets, shrines or other receptacles for keeping or exhibiting sacred relics).

Contrait 1108, 1121, 1165: the cripple, the lame.

Cordine 448: curtain(bed), tapestry.

Crisne 429: hair.

Defaé 417: infidel, faithless.

Deffremer 302: to open.

Deflorés 264: deflowered (=deprived of virginity, violated).

Delaier 198: to leave.

Depané 410, 428; Depanee 973: torn, torn to pieces.

Despensier 671, 700, 759: dispensator= the newly appointed officer administering to the needs of Saint Alexis.

Destaindre 1122: to alleviate, appease.

Destor 121: hidden place, secluded place.

Enerbi 450: uninhabited, desolate.

Enferté 1105: infirmity, illness.

Engigneör 1207: the Devil (=the supreme deceiver).

Engoulés 33: bordered, adorned with a fur collar.

Enpoindre 108: to direct, fix on.

Entrafier 146: to pledge in marriage, betroth.

Escacier 194 (Picard form): to hide, shake (=loose from).

Esclarier 476: to enlighten (=to supply with spiritual light).

Euwist 73 (=*euist*): imperfect subj. 3 of *avoir*.

Favrechier 1168: to forge, fashion (with a hammer).

Fievé 73: enfeoffed.

Forceur 186: stronger, greater.

Frestraus 151: a kind of medieval flute or flageolet.

Gige 152: a medieval stringed instrument resembling the mandolin used by the minstrels.

Govrener 937, 1000: to take care of, manage.

Grigois 791, 1169: Greek.

Hascie 9: anguish, torment.

Hate 1060 (=*haute*).

Herbrigier 481, 597, 613, etc.: to lodge, shelter, find lodging.

Iaus 43, 786 (*Illos*), personal pron., tonic form: them.

Kuit 795, 1168: prepared by fire or heat to render the gold more malleable.

Lagne 718: any woollen garment (id est, a coarse woollen shirt worn as a penance, a hair
    shirt; cf. Oxford MS.: *en sa haire*).

Laisor 1164: leisure, opportunity.

Le 305, 335, 338, etc. (Picard form for *la*), pers.pr., fem., her, it.

Le 75, 166, 871, 1082 (Picard form for *la*), def.art., fem.

Leus 111, 352, 622: then, at once.

Leuvier 273; Leuwiers 684: reward, recompense.

Liu 450, 592, 659: place.

Mar 296 (*mala hora*), adverb: wrongly, in an evil hour.

Millor 116, 1206: better.

Mireör 1201: mirror; *se faire mireör de* 1201: to become the mirror (model) of . . .,
    id est, to imitate perfectly the model of Saint Alexis.

Monaé 354; Monoie 1137: coined money; *un denier monaé* 354: a coined denarius.

Mos 1004 (=*Mors*).

No 419 (=*nostre*).

Orgener 152: to sing.

Paile 67, 361 (=*pale*).

Paine 71, 253, 1149, 1154, etc.: Picard form of *peine*.

Palasin 709: palatine.

Pamier 605, 679 (=*paumier*)

Pangne 328 (=*paine* 71, etc., q.v.).

Pasmisons 1059 (=*pasmoison*).

Patonier 834 (=*pautonier*).

Peuc 845, 1033: preterite 1 of *pooir*.

Poc 836, 1022: preterite 1 of *pooir*.

Provendier 672: the poor ones who come for provender, id est, the alms-receivers.

Puslent 237: stinking, foul.

Quariaus 588: bolt from a cross-bow.

Ralumer 1121: to recover one's sight.

Reng 401: present 1 of *rendre*.

Roé 32: ornamented with circular figures (wheels or rings), pattened with rose-work.

Romoisin 506: sou (gold coin) from the county of Rouen.

Rote 151: a medieval stringed instrument, sort of harp or cittern with 5 strings, used by
    the Breton and Welsh minstrels in singing their lays.

Saisir 113: to put in legal possession of; seize (929).

Sami 449, 794; Samit 1094: samite (a heavy rich silk fabric, interwoven with gold or silver).

Satier 832, 1159 (=*sautier*).

Se 464 (=Picard form for Francien *sa*).

Siel 307 (=*ciel*).

Sieut 822 (=*seut*): Preterite 3 of *soloir*.

Sisent 157: preterite 6 of *seoir*.

Siuwe 528 (=*soie*).

So 145; Sou 307 (=*sous*).

Sodoier 683: soldier (of Christ).

Solaus 855: sun.

Sonc; *par sonc l'abe* 744, 842: at the break of dawn, at dawn.

Sougretain 522, 531, 552: sacristan, sexton.

Suer 224: dear friend (term of endearment).

Suiier 343: to follow.

Tafur 679, 834: wretch, vagabond, heathen.

Tainst 914 (=*taint*).

Tapin; *a tapin* 497, 705: disguised, in secret (705).

Tors 1071, 1084 (=*tos*);

Trestorné; *ja nen iert trestorné* 878: without fail.

Trinus 398: three.

Vai 605, 787 (=*vait*).

Vasel 1090: coffin.

Vesque 873: bishop.

Veveté 1056: widow.

Viele 150: viol (a medieval stringed instrument, a sort of fiddle).

Vise 239 (=*vice*)

Vo 226, 241, 281 (=*vostre*).

Ydrope 1122: those suffering from dropsy.

Ymne 1158: hymn.

Ytrope 1108 (see *ydrope*).

II. RELATIONSHIP OF THE PARIS MS. (BIBL. NAT.,
   FR. 2162) OF THE *VIE DE SAINT ALEXIS*
   TO ITS LATIN SOURCE[1]

The source of our 13th century Old French poem is the Latin prose legend entitled "Vita S. Alexii Confessoris" and published in the *Acta Sanctorum Bollandiorum*, July, IV, pp. 251-253. (See Appendix, pp. 149-153.)
The first thing which stands out as we compare the two texts is that our OF poem (1224 vv.) is a greatly amplified version of its Latin model[2]. In the following pages, by means of several comparisons, I shall endeavor to show that: (1) our poet does not blindly follow his Latin source; rather, in many places, especially relating the dialogues of the young couple and the long laments following the death of Saint Alexis, he skillfully manipulated his material to give it an original form; (2) he has framed the retelling of the Latin *Vita* according to the tradition of Medieval Latin poetics (i.e. he has followed the three-part scheme of poetic composition: *exordium, narratio, conclusio*) attesting a firm notion of how a poem should be constructed.

Exordium

Just how closely did our poet follow his Latin model? Laisses I and II (vv. 1-25) must be attributed to the poet, for their content is entirely missing from the Latin *Vita*. They serve as the *exordium* of our poem in which the author endeavors to make his hearers favorably disposed to what he has to say. He appeals to them to be attentive and describes the life of this most holy man who devoted himself completely to the service of God[3].

---

1 See my critical edition of this 13th century version of the *Vie de Saint Alexis* which precedes this article.
2 The variant MS. *O* (located in Oxford, Bodl., Canonici misc. 74) contains 1043 verses. See my complete edition of the Oxford MS. (*O*) which has just appeared in *Romania*, Tome 92 (1971), pp. 1-36. Cf. the 11th century version which contains 625 vv. All verse references pertaining to the 11th century version which appear on some of the following pages are taken from Gaston Paris, *La Vie de Saint Alexis*, 7th ed. (Paris, 1966).
3 It is a well established fact that Medieval Latin poetics placed great emphasis on the techniques of the *exordium* and *conclusio*. See E. R. Curtius, „Zur Interpretation des Alexiusliedes", *ZrP*, LVI (1936), 117. For a fuller treatment, see Curtius,

Narratio

The second part of our poetic composition, the narration, follows quite closely the legend. However, three greatly amplified passages (the separation scene, the lament scenes, and the procession-interment scene) deserve special consideration. The first two most effectively illustrate our poet's creativity in his handling of the Latin source. The third is a fine example of how our author has utilized several of the conventional medieval means of amplifying a text[4].

The Separation Scene

The effective use of *descriptio* by our poet in Laisse VII (the bedroom, the bed, the physical beauty of the virgin, etc.)[5] to emphasize the singular steadfastness of Alexis in renouncing these carnal temptations sent by the Devil makes the separation scene which follows between the young couple (comprising most of Laisses VIII, IX and X) all the more moving. We feel the poignant struggle being waged in Alexis' soul. How much more human and touching is the scene as it unfolds in our poem: the maiden converses tenderly with Alexis (she is conspicuously mute in the *Vita*). Her beauty is almost irresistible (vv. 185-88): »Et la virgine ert tant belle, qui le vist blancoiier/ El lit u elle atent son forceur desirier/ Molt euist cuer de piere u de fer u d'acier/ Cui ne presist talent del siecle a asaiier.« (In the *Vita*, no mention whatsoever is made of her physical features.) She is visibly moved and grief stricken (as is Alexis):

> Quant cele li ceurt sus, sel prent a acoler,
> Entre ses bras la dame se commenche a pasmer.   304
> Quant le voit li sains hons, si commenche a plorer,
> Ja veïsiés tel duel quant vint a desevrer;
> Il n'a sou siel nul home tant peuist sermoner
> Qui vos desist awan, tant se peuist pener,   308
> Le duel qu'ele demaine quant l'en voit aler.

European Literature and the Latin Middle Ages, trans. by Willard R. Trask (New York and Evanston, 1962), Parts 3, 4 and 5. Cf. E. Faral, *Les Arts poétiques du XIIe et du XIIIe siècles* (Paris, 1962), Chap. I.

4 As was the case with medieval writers, most of the originality of our poet is found in his use of the conventional means of amplifying a text. Among the predominate devices of amplification employed by our author throughout the poem are: *descriptio, repetitio, interpretatio, expolitio, imago,* and *exclamatio.*

5 The description of the nuptial chamber and of the young bride does not occur in the *Vita.* Cf.: „Vespere autem facto dixit Euphemianus filio suo: Intra, fili, in cubiculum, & visita sponsam tuam. Ut autem intravit, coepit nobilissimus juvenis, & in Christo sapientissimus instruere sponsam suam . . ."

This passage illustrates best the most salient difference between the two texts. Our poet has gone out of his way to bring out in relief Alexis' "humanity" as well as his sanctity. His character is much more fully developed. In the *Vita*, no real attempt has been made to develop Alexis' character as a man. We are merely given a dry account of the events which have transpired[6].

This scene depicting the unrest in Alexis' soul as he prepares to leave the paternal house[7] should be compared with Alexis' 17 years spent in the same house after his providential return to Rome. His steadfastness in refusing to console his grieving parents and spouse is so exceptional that our poet remarks in vv. 652-53: »Esmervilier s'en puet tote crestïentés,/ Comment il puet si estre en son cuer adurés[8]. How far Alexis has progressed in his "imitatio Christi!" Gone is the poignant struggle between his most tender and natural feelings and his adherence to God's call. He has sacrificed all natural ties to what he conceives to be his duty to God. The worlds of Alexis and of his parents can never be bridged, for one has his eyes fixed on the heavenly future, the other on the distant past, to their Alexis, the son of Euphemian, who no longer exists. Both are engrossed in their own unrelenting program: one of self-abnegation, the other of sterile lamentations. Therefore, not only does Alexis' filial insensitivity stand out in this scene, but also the parental callousness of the mother and father who are oblivious to the appalling conditions enveloping the saint, their very own son, whom they frequently see before them.

---

6 The creativity of our poet in his handling of this scene is all the more apparent when one compares it with that of the 11th century version:

Com vit le lit, esguardat la pulcele,   56
Donc li remembret de son seignour celeste,
Que plus at chier que tote rien terrestre:
»E! Deus,« dist il, »si forz pechiez m'apresset!
S'or ne m'en fui, molt criem que ne t'en perde.«   60

Once Alexis sees the reclining figure of his young bride on the bed (symbol of the sensual pleasures of this world), he is seized by a sudden illumination. Henceforward, his love of God will be the only motivating force in his life. There is no real hesitation, no vacillation on his part, no poignant struggle in his soul. On the contrary, he is impatient to depart: "Mais lui ert tart qued il s'en fust tornez« (v. 65).

7 In the beginning of Laisse VIII, the reader feels the veritable anguish of our saint, torn between filial duty and affection and divine calling. Alexis knows that his departure will cause great grief to his mother and father and he loves them dearly: »Molt par est anguoseus selonc ço que il sent, / Car s'il s'en fuit de Rome, bien set a ensïent / Grant duel fera son pere et sa mere ensement;« (vv. 201-203).

8 Those who accuse Alexis of heartlessness, cruelty and ingratitude have failed to comprehend God's ways and just what is really involved here. Once an individual has been selected by God to become one of his special few (i.e. a saint), and the former accepts that calling, he must henceforward go all the way in his »imitatio Christi.« His saintly program must entail a complete surrender of himself to God, a complete severance with the ephemeral things of this world which could impede his spiritual growth. He must die unto himself, sever all natural bonds, and systematically reduce

The Lament Scenes

The two mourning scenes (the first after the departure of Alexis, the second after his death), in conjunction with the touching separation scene, best attest the fact that our poet did not blindly follow his Latin source. Rather, the symmetrically constructed speeches depicting the grief of the parents and bride (wherein he employs many of the conventional means of *amplificatio*), all attest the conscious, creative work of a talented artist conversant with the theory and practice of medieval poetics.

The sequence of the mourning scenes, throughout the entire poem, is invariably the same: first the father, then the mother, then the maiden. In the laments of the parents and bride after the departure of Alexis, our poem differs noticeably from the *Vita* both in content and in emphasis. In the *Vita*, only the mother and bride lament and their grief is much more subdued:

> Mater quoque ejus a die, qua discessit suus filius, sternens saccum in pavimento cubiculi sui, sedensque super illud ejulans, & lamentans dicebat: Vivit Dominus, quia ita manebo, donec cognoscam, quid actum sit de filio meo. Sponsa vero ejus dixit ad socrum suam: Non egrediar de domo tua, sed similabo me turturi[9], quae omnino alteri non copulatur, dum ejus socius captus fuerit; sic & ego faciam, quousque sciam, quid factum sit de dulcissimo conjuge meo.

What really stands out in our poem is the utter self-centeredness of the parents. They do not truly love the child for himself. Rather, their love is concentrated

---

his ego until he achieves perfect conformity with the Divine Will. The life of a saint is nothing else but the progressive victory of the supernatural over the natural. Everything else must be subordinated to it: love of family, terrestrial goods, glory, etc.: »Qui plus aime ne pere ne mere ne parent, / Fil ne mollier ne terre, honor ne casement / Que moi, dist nostre Sires, ne mon commandement, / Il n'est dignes de moi ne a moi ne s'atent.« (vv. 207-210). See Anna Granville Hatcher, »The Old-French poem St. Alexis: A Mathematical Demonstration,« *Traditio*, VIII (1952), 120-121. The saint, like the epic hero, cannot be judged by the common yardstick and pressed into the common mold of mankind. The only thing that matters is the ultimate victory, the salvation of his immortal soul. But he is not selfishly egocentric, devoid of human feelings. In our text, the poet has certainly stressed the human aspects of Alexis (in the separation scene): his suffering, his poignant struggle in leaving those he loves. This is perhaps the most salient feature of our poem. But, even in the 11th century version where the poignancy of the separation is not stressed, Alexis has not cruelly forgotten his family. Though impatient to leave, he generously lingers a while to impress upon his young wife the Truth which has just been revealed to him: »La mortel vide li prist molt a blasmer, / De la celeste li mostrat veritet« (vv. 63-4). And later, through his efficacious intercession, he procures for them all eternal glory in paradise, the only reason for the sojourn of any Christian here on earth (See stanzas CXXI and CXXII).

9 This comparison with the turtle-dove does not occur in our text until v. 1079 of Laisse LIV. Cf. vv. 421-481, wherein the entire household participates in the lament and the grief of all is much more intense.

on a selfish enjoyment and use of Alexis. Being untouched by grace, they are unable to comprehend the vocation of their son. Such parents are indeed to be pitied as they express their bereavement, since their entire world (i.e., their worldly plans for Alexis) is coming apart before their eyes. Euphemian wants an heir, someone to continue the family tradition. He bestows everything on the child (fine education, servants, luxuries, etc.), but ignores completely, throughout the entire poem, the inner needs of his only son. His role is that of the veritable "paterfamilias" who is forever blind to the ironic fact that God did grant to him and his wife a son truly "a son talent;" one who would scorn the transitory things of this life and devote himself completely to his heavenly Father by means of a perfect "imitatio Christi." The father's wishes and plans inevitably had to be frustrated. And what greater reward was awaiting Alexis: All the representatives of Christendom and of terrestrial power (the Pope, the Emperors, the Roman people) bestow honor and glory upon him at the end.

And what about the mother? She is perhaps the blindest of all. Her maternal love is concentrated on the purely physical aspects[10]. She has lost the son whom she had borne and carried in her womb (v. 577 of the Oxford MS. expresses it well: "Ne sa mere Glael ke fust sa portuure"). Hence the greater passion and violence of her grief which prepares us for her unmotherly scene of anger after the death and recognition of Alexis. She had been given an opportunity, as it were, of "imitatio Mariae" but is completely oblivious to the spiritual calling of her son. In the midst of such parents, what other choice did Alexis have but to leave? The words of Saint Bernard of Clairvaux (Ep. 322.2), exhorting the true Christian to flee his family without pity, are so appropriate: »Ipsi sunt qui non te diligunt, sed gaudium ex te.« (Quoted by Anna Granville Hatcher, p. 128).

The second lament of the parents and bride (vv. 912-1087) is the longest scene in our poem and merits closer attention. The second half of Laisse XLV (vv. 912-919) to verse 964 of Laisse XLVIII are based on lines 137-146 of the *Vita* ("Ephemianus . . . ponam," which terminates Part 9). In vv. 912-931, our poet describes the violent reaction of the father after Ethio had read the "cartre." Our poem follows the *Vita* very closely in depicting the extreme grief and despair of Euphemian:

Euphemianus autem pater ejus, ut audivit verba chartae, factus exanimis cecidit in terram, & surgens scidit vestimenta sua, coepitque canos capitis sui evellere, barbam trahere, atque semetipsum discerpere: & corruens super ipsum corpus clamabat[11]:

---

10 See Anna Granville Hatcher, p. 128.
11 Cf. the 11th century version which summarizes this scene in one line: »Quant ot li pedre ço que dit at la chartre, / Ad ambes mains deromt sa blanche barbe:« (vv. 386-7).

Though *descriptio* is the main source of amplification, several effective examples of *imago* (not found in the *Vita*) occur:

Ausi tainst comme cendre et enpali le vis (v. 914).
Si com hons forsenés a la presse partie (v. 924).
Ensement se depane comme cose esmarie (v. 926).

In the lament of the father which takes up the rest of these laisses (vv. 932-963)[12], our poet has intercalated one very important verse: »Plus te desire m'arme que dou mont l'onoranche« (v. 962). In a speech replete with egotistical laments, the father, in this one line, shows for the first time an awareness of his son's true calling and the reasons behind his strange behavior[13].
This spiritual illumination makes his own comportment appear even more selfish, an effect evidently desired by the author. Note also the effective use of *exclamatio* (plus *interpretatio*) in v. 961: »Et Mors, por coi te targes, por coi fais demorance . . .«
The last two lines of Laisse XLVIII (vv. 965-6) and Laisses XLIX-LI (vv. 967-1052) are based on lines 147 (beginning of Part 10) to the second word on line 162 and are devoted to the death lament of the mother. As in the Latin *Vita*, what really stands out in these laisses is her utter egotism. The passage is replete with her self-pitying lamentations. She commences her lament with an appeal to the Roman people: »E car me faites voie, bone gens honoree!«/ Si vera la caitive sa dure destinee,/ La dolereuse portee dont ja n'iert confortee« (vv. 978-980). Her spiritual blindness is the most pronounced of all. Not in the slightest degree does she comprehend God's will. Nor does she seem to want to. She even goes so far as to blame God for her grief and blindness: »Et Diex,

---

12 Once again we have present the stylistic device of symmetrically constructed speeches. The sequence of the mourning scene is the same: father, mother, maiden. Approximately 3 laisses are devoted to each of the laments.
13 No such spiritual awareness occurs in the *Vita*:
»Heu me Domine (Deus) meus, quare mihi sic fecisti, & quare ita contristasti animam meam, & per tot annos suspiria, & gemitus incussisti mihi? Ego enim sperabam aliquando audire vocem tuam, & de te agnitum habere, ubicumque esses, & nunc video te custodem senecturis meae in grabato jacentem, & mihi non loquentem. Heu me! qualem consolationem in corde meo ponam?«
In the 11th century version, even greater emphasis is placed on the spiritual blindness of Euphemian. Nowhere in the poem is his role of the paterfamilias more vividly portrayed (See vv. 401-3 and stanzas LXXXIII-IV). He is so spiritually blind that, in v. 410, he asks for Alexis' forgiveness (»Filz, la toue aneme seit el ciel assolude.«) at the moment that his son is experiencing his greatest triumph and glory in God's very presence. And what supreme irony emerges from the following verse: »A! las, pechables, com par fui avogles!« (v. 394). He accuses himself for his past blindness, but is not his present lament an even greater confirmation of his present blindness? There is not reflected one iota of spiritual illumination in the father's entire speech and, as in the *Vita*, he is still completely oblivious to the meaning and purpose of his son's life.

76

por coi faisoies si mon cuer esmarir/ Et mon cuer aveuler que ainc ne peuc coisir/ Que ce fust Alexis, mes fix, dont voi marir?« (vv. 1032-34)[14]. She thinks only of herself throughout the entire lament and heaps reproach after reproach upon her son, e.g.: »Trop par euis dur cuer ne sai que je t'en mente« (v. 1011).

Diex, com le pot souffrir nus hons de ta jovente,	1012
Quant veöies ton pere et ta mere plorente	
Et t'espeuse la belle qui por toi se demente,	
C'ainc ne nos confortas? Molt euis dure entente.	
Isi grant cruaté ja mais Diex ne consente,	1016
»E fix,« ce dist la mere, »comment le puis sofrir	
Que cascun jor veöies tant plor et tant sospir	1026
De ton pere et de moi qui t'aviëns nourit?«	

Unlike both the *Vita* and the 11th century poem, the theme of the »pater-familias« occurs several times in the mother's lament, e.g.: »Sire en deuissiés estre!« (v. 993). »Or deuisses, biax fix, maintenir t'espousee,/ Ton pere conforter, ta mere l'esgaree,/ Et govrener deuisses ta maisnie privee.« (vv. 998-1000).
As in the 11th century version, little pity for Alexis' physical distress is shown by the mother. She does, in a few lines, express concern for the physical suffering of her son (See vv. 993-96 and 1028-31), but it is always related to her own self pity. Cf. lines 157-162 of the *Vita*:

Plorate mecum omnes, qui adestis; quia decem & septem annos eum in domo mea habui, & non cognovi, quod unicus filius meus esset, sed servi ejus injuriabant, alapis percutiebant eum, & sputa in faciem ejus jactabant. Heu me! Quis dabit oculis meis fontem lachrymarum? ut plangam die, ac nocte dolorem animae meae.

Various figures of diction and figures of thought are employed by the author to illustrate some of these themes, among others:

1) *imago*, e.g.
»Comme beste savage qui soit descainee« (v. 972)
»Et ensi crië et brait comme riens forseenee« (v. 975)
»Tainte est si comme cendre et roide et abosmee« (v. 982)
»A haute vois escrië comme feme dervee« (v' 987)

---

14 In the *Vita*, no direct reproaches are heaped upon God, but the mother's reaction is just as violent and physical. She is utterly selfish and does not care one bit about Alexis. His death simply left her with an empty womb (See p. 75). And how vividly are the claims of the womb presented in the following passage: »Date mihi viri Dei aditum, ut videam consolationem animae meae, ut videam filium meum, qui suxit ubera mea.«

2) *interpretatio*, e. g.
»Et ensi crïe et brait« (v. 975)
»Ensi pleure et gaimente« (v. 968)
»Triste et dolente« (v. 1007)

3) *descriptio*, e. g.
»De tote sa vesture a a ses mains depanee,
Sanglante sa maiselle, tote est descevelee,
Et ensi crïe et brait comme riens forseenee,«
(vv. 973-75)

It is obvious that in all three laments, many traditional gestures of grief are
used by the author, especially relating to the tearing of one's beard, hair, clothing; swoons, recovery, etc.: »A ambes mains detrait sa barbe o le poil gris,/
Trestot son vestement a desront et malmis,« (vv. 917-18). »Sa teste la cenue
et sa barbe florie/ Desront a ambes mains et son cors martir[i]e,« (vv. 922-23).
»De tote sa vesture a a ses mains depanee,/ Sanglante sa maiselle, tote est
descevelee,« (vv. 973-4); etc. However, even a superficial reading of the text
suffices to reveal that our poet has not blindly and systematically utilized these
topoi, but has demonstrated originality and creativity in exceeding their conventional scope, e.g.:

Tant fort baise le cors u ke le puet sentir,
La ciere angelial que tant voit resplendir,   1038
Et enbrache le cors la u le voit gesir,
A poi que ne se tue c'om ne le puet tenir.

4) *exclamatio*, e. g.:
»E Mos! car me prenés . . .« (v. 1004)

Laisses LII-LIV (vv. 1053-1087) are based on only 5 lines of the *Vita* (the
second word on line 162 through line 166, end of Part 10) and are devoted to
the lament of the bride. It is obvious that our poem is considerably more
bride-oriented than its pope-centered Latin model[15].
The lament of the maiden is much more tender and subdued than the two
preceding ones, the only one that touches our hearts. She has not yet grasped
the significance of Alexis' program of perfect »imitatio Christi[16].«

---

15 See (in both texts) the separation scene between Alexis and his young bride which
best attests this point.
16 The *Vita* highlights her spiritual blindness. Cf.: Heu me! quia hodie desolata sum,
& apparui vidua. Jam non habeo in quem aspiciam, nec in quem oculos levem. Nunc
ruptum est speculum meum, & periit spes mea; amodo coepit dolor, qui finem non
habet.
In the 11th century version, she also has not become spiritually enlightened to the
point of comprehending God's will. However, she does vaguely recognize the "neces-
sity" of Alexis' saintly program and admits, in the midst of her lamentations, that it
would have been »felonie« and »lastét« for him to return to her in the role of bridegroom (See vv. 471-75).

Her opening lament reveals this:

»Sire,« ce dist s'espeuse, »com or sui desperee!
Molt ai fait longe atente et dure desiree,   1066
Dolente moi caitive et veve et esgaree,
Je cuidoi[e] encore estre aucun jor confortee.
Mais ce n'en iert ja mais, tel est ma destinee,
Quant cis ne me conforte cui je sui esposee,   1070
De cui je deuisse estre a tos jors honoree.«

In this stanza the maiden appears just as spiritually blind as the parents. But is
this not the spontaneous emotional outburst of a grieving loving wife as she
gazes, for the first time after 34 years, upon the dead body of her beloved
husband? She is once again the sensual young bride, reclining on the nuptial
bed, awaiting her husband: »Or puis mais dire que ma joie est alee,/ Car ne
serai ja mais de ses iex esgardee,/ Ne ne sera ma bouche a la soie privee.«
(vv. 1072-74). But does she remain completely spiritually unenlightened? Have
all the »biax sermons« of Alexis in Laisse VIII exhorting her to flee the false
joys of this earth and to devote herself to a higher bridegroom (»Dieu espeuse
soiés,« v. 240. »Cascun jor en vo cuer aiés ramembrement./ Del grant espeuse
celeste qui el ciel nos atent,« vv. 241-2) gone for nought? Though she does
not turn directly to God[17], she is, nevertheless, obeying Alexis' very exhortat-
ions as vv. 1077-84 (especially v. 1082) bear out:

»Amis,« ce dist s'espeuse, »or sui venue a jor
Que trestote ma joie est mue en tristor.
A loi de toterele qui eskive verdor,
Deduirai mais mon cors et vivrai en labor,   1080
N'escouterai mais cant ne ne porterai flor,
Ne desir mais del siecle le joie ne l'onor.
A tos jors arai mais vest[e]üre de plor,
Tors jors serai mais veve, n'ai soing d'atre signor.«   1084

It would seem quite likely, as in the 11th century version[18], that Alexis' life of

---

17 In the *Vita*, God is totally absent and the egocentrism of the bride is stressed (See
   footnote 21). Cf. stanza XCIX (vv. 491-95) of the 11th century version wherein she
   does turn directly to God:
   »Or sui jo vedve,« dist la pulcele,
   »Ja mais ledece n'avrai, quer ne puet estre,
   Ne charnel ome n'avrai ja mais en terre.
   Deu servirai, le rei qui tot governet:
   Il nem faldrat, s'il veit que jo lui serve.«
18 Cf. stanza CXXII (vv. 606-610):
   Sainz Alexis est el ciel senz dotance,
   Ensemble o Deu, en la compaigne as angeles,
   O la pulcele dont se fist si estranges;
   Or l'at o sei, ensemble sont lour anemes:
   Ne vos sai dire com lour ledece est grande.

complete self-abnegation eventually resulted in their union in heaven and the granting of his prayer: »Et Diex, quant jugera le siecle a jugement,/ Nos doinst ensanble glorie, el ciel herbrigement.« (vv. 246-7).

The Procession-Interment Scene

The procession-interment scene (vv. 1088-1185) is based on lines 167 of the *Vita*, beginning of Part 11, to "plenum," line 184. *Repetitio, interpretatio* and *expolitio* are the predominate devices of amplification. Our poem follows its Latin source closely: The holy body of Saint Alexis is wrapped in rich silken sheets, placed in a beautifully decorated coffin, and transported to the church of Saint Boniface where it is honored in great pomp and majesty for seven days. It is placed in a magnificent sepulchre of gold and precious stones and laid to rest. Then there arises from the tomb a heavenly fragrance with miraculous healing powers.

As in the *Vita*, in these laisses and in the remaining ones, the family of Saint Alexis is conspicuous by its complete absence[19]. Not one verse, not one single word, is devoted to anyone of them. A new movement has commenced, that of the "holy joy" theme which differs so radically from the preceding passages of grief and despair with which the parents and bride are so intimately associated. Their spiritual blindness has excluded them from taking part in it. Their absolute program of sterile lamentations has been replaced by one of extreme jubilation, of songs of praise and thanksgiving to God. Unlike the parents, the Pope, the Emperors and the Roman people comprehend the meaning and purpose of Saint Alexis' life; and God shows his approval by working numerous miracles and wonders in his name.

Though in other passages the aforementioned devices of amplification frequently serve no function other than to fill in a hemistich[20], they are effectiv-

---

19 Our poem (and the *Vita*) differs noticeably from the 11th century version in this respect. In the latter, the Pope, amazed at the outbursts of grief still being displayed by the family (instead of rejoicing and honoring Alexis at this his greatest hour) rebukes them for their fixed spiritual blindness and proclaims that the time has now come for jubilation:

»Seignour, que faites?« ço dist li apostolies.
»Que valt cist criz, cist duels ne ceste noise?
Cui que seit duels, a nostre ues est il joie;
Quer par cestui avroms bon adjutorie;
Si li preioms que de toz mals nos tolget.«
(vv. 501-505.)

Both poets, each in his own particular way, get their point across: the time for rejoicing has commenced and all estrange themselves from the family's grief which fades away into the distant background.

20 A notable exception occurs in Laisse XXXIII. Our poet uses *repetitio* (vv. 702-712) not so much as a device of amplification, but to give more force to this brief narration

ely utilized here to bring out in relief: (1) the miraculous healing powers of
»l'homme de Dieu,« e. g.:

Nus hons n'aproisme a cors de si grant enferté
Que par main ne l'ait Diex et garit et sané.　　　　1106
Assés i ot le jor aveules ralumés
Et contrait redrechié, y trope desenflé;
Li sourt i ont oï et li müel parlé,
De maint cors d'ome i sont li dÿable jeté,　　　　1110
Tote ont le jor perdue illuec lor poësté.

Contrais salir de joie, aveules ralumer
Et les ardans destaindre, ydrope desenfler　　　　1122
Por le merite al saint, et les muiaus parler.

As malades saner, as contrais redrecier　　　　　1165

Car il i sont le jor malade maint sané.　　　　　1185

Et sane les malades et jete de languor,
Les aveules ralume, les contrais rent valor　　　　1190

(2) the immense throng and the ardor of the common people to touch Alexis
(disdaining »Et argent et monoies et besans d'outre mer« scattered on the
streets by the treasurer of the Emperors)[21], e. g.:

of Alexis' life. On this point, he has simply imitated the Latin source. Cf. both texts:
　　Puis a tote sa vie escripte en latin,
　　Com le nori ses peres jovenchiel et meskin
　　Et il li quist mollier des filles Constentin,
　　Et com il s'en fui fors del regne a tapin
　　Et ala par la terre a loi de pelerin,
　　Et com fu a Rohais el regne barbarin
　　Et reçuit les amosnes a la gent de son lin,
　　En la maison son pere le riche palasin
　　Estuit .XVII. ans c'ainc ne gosta de vin,
　　Ne ne se fist conoistre n'a parent n'a cousin,
　　N'a mere n'a mollier, n'a viellart n'a mescin.

　　& scripsit per ordinem omnem vitam suam,
　　qualiter respuerit nuptias, & qualiter
　　conversatus fuerit in peregrinatione,
　　qualiterque contra voluntatem suam redierit
　　Romam, & domo patris sui opprobria multa sustinuerit.
Note that in the 11th century version, the story of Alexis' life is succinctly related in
one line: »Com s'en alat e come il s'en revint.« (v. 285). This single verse, however,
encompasses all of the 34 years which Saint Alexis devoted to his »imitatio Christi«
(the figure 34 being undoubtedly based on the 33 and approximately one third years
that Christ spent on this earth).
21 The Roman people, for this moment at least, are able to imitate the scorn of Alexis
for the ephemeral things of this world. And what a sweet victory for Saint Alexis, for

Tot le keurent veöir, car molt l'ont desiré;
Tant i akeurent gent de par la grant cité
Que molt fu grans la presse quant furent asamblé.   1104

Mais tant est grans la presse, nus hons n'i puet aler;   1128
Qui la veïst la gent de partot asanler,
Acorir par ces rues et a cors arester
Et la biere baisier qui tant i puet presser
Qu'il i puist aprochier ne ses mains adeser,   1132
La peuist on mervelles de ses iex regarder.

Li empereör voient le grant peule asanler   1134
Et a la gent menue si grant presse mener,
Lor tresoriers commandent deniers a aporter
Et argent et monoies et besans d'outre mer;
Par les rues le font aprés lor dos jeter,   1138
Par les deniers se cuident del peule delivrer,
Mais nïent ne lor vaut quank'il i font jeter,
Car por l'avoir ne vellent povre gent retorner.

Tant par fu grans la presse et li bruis de la gent
C'om lor fait par ces rues jeter or et argent
Por la presse partir, mais ne lor vaut noient,   1144
Que tant par sont trestuit vers le saint cors entent,
Ne presisent deniers por tot l'or d'orïent.

La veïsiés le peule en molt grant desirier
Devant le cors orer et la biere baisier,
Ces dras terdre a lor iex qui s'en puet asier!
Or a cascuns laisor qu'il s'en puet aaisier   1164

Conclusio

The real conclusion commences only with verse 1202. The first part of
Laisse LX culminates the "holy joy" theme. This is a scene of jubilation and
thanksgiving to Jesus (»Qui si lor a muee en joie lor tristor«)[22] by having sent
to them such a great and efficacious gift, that of His holy instrument and
servant, Saint Alexis.
Verses 1195-1201 (wherein Saint Alexis' intercession is sought by the Roman
people for those who have fallen into mortal sin: »es mains a souduitor«)
serve as introduction to the real conclusion[23].

---

the greatest accomplishment of the saint is perhaps the example which he has left
behind. Cf. the parents' inability to see beyond their selfish grief in order to comprehend God's message and purpose.

22 The text of the Oxford manuscript terminates here.

The first part of the conclusion (vv. 1202-1208) is what we might refer to as an edifying *conclusio*: By following the example of Saint Alexis, we can become spiritually better, thus freeing ourselves from the bonds of Satan so as to attain heaven. In verses 1209-1224, the edifying *conclusio* has changed into a prayer: Saint Alexis and all the saints in heaven are directly invoked by the Roman people and asked to pray for them before the sight of God so that they might, on the terrible Day of Judgment, be united with the blessed in paradise.

It is apparent that: (1) our poet has not followed like a timid translator his Latin source. Rather, in two greatly amplified passages (the separation scene and the lament scenes) we must give him credit for skillfully manipulating his material to give it an original form. In the touching separation scene, great stress is placed on Alexis' "humanity" as well as his sanctity. This enables his character to be more fully developed than in the *Vita*. In the lament scenes, our poet has gone out of his way to bring out in relief the inability of the parents and bride to divorce themselves from their personal grief in order to comprehend God's will. He also contrasts their egocentric comportment with Alexis' complete severance with all natural bonds and systematic reduction of his ego to achieve perfect conformity with the Divine Will. (2) he was well versed in the theory and practice of Medieval Latin poetics. His effective use of many of the conventional means of *amplificatio* is especially evident in the procession-interment scene. The symmetrical construction of the two framing parts (the *exordium* contains 25 vv., the *conclusio* 23) is characteristic of our text as I have endeavored to show in the *narratio*[24]. Though our poem does not conform rigidly to architectonic laws of proportion, its author manifests throughout most of the poem a fine sensitivity for balancing corresponding parts, an accomplishment which distinguishes him quite radically from the poets of the preceding two centuries[25].

---

23 The *Vita* terminates here. Cf.:
      Tunc populi jocundantes, maximas Domino gratias agebant,
      qui tale populo suo conferre dignatus est subsidium,
      per quod omnis quicumque sincera mentis intentione
      deprecatus fuerit, petitionis effectum sine dubio consequatur.
      Per Dominum nostrum.
24 See, in particular, the symmetrically constructed lament scenes.
25 See Curtius, „Zur Interpretation des Alexiusliedes," pp. 117-118.

III. A CRITICAL EDITION OF THE FOURTEENTH
     CENTURY OLD FRENCH POEM VERSION OF THE
     VIE DE SAINT ALEXIS

INTRODUCTION

In the present edition of this Old French version of the *Vie de saint Alexis*,
I have made numerous references, particularly in the linguistic section and in
the Notes, not only to the ever-popular 11th century version and the *Vita*
(the Latin prose legend), but also to the greatly neglected 13th century version[1].
A comparative study, both linguistic and thematic, of all the main Old French
versions of the *Vie de saint Alexis* is now readily available, for the first time,
to scholars interested in hagiography and specifically in one of the most popular
of all medieval legends[2].
The great bulk of the research done on the Alexis legend has concentrated on
the 11th century version, very interesting and informative with regard to the
primitive language and rigid architectonic construction, a veritable medieval
gem in these respects, but vastly inferior, at least in my opinion, to the more
artistic and humanly sensitive 13th century version[3].
The text, composed in the early fourteenth century (1330), in octosyllabic
rhymed couplets, is preserved in two manuscripts, both written in a fine
legible hand, and located in Paris at the Bibl. nat.: MS. 244 de la ville d'Avranches, fol. 72a-79d, which served as the base manuscript of this critical edition
and MS. 6835, nouv. acq. fr., ancien Ashburnham, Appendix 175, fol. 52d-
58d.
To the best of my knowledge, this critical edition is preceded only by E. Walberg's good edition contained in *Contes pieux en vers du XIVe siècle, tirés du*

---

1 See the Introduction of my critical edition of the 13th century version.
2 The extreme popularity of the Alexis legend throughout the entire Middle Ages,
  in innumerable versions (Besides the Syriac, Greco-Latin, German, English and
  French Lives of Saint Alexis, there are many other versions: numerous Provencal,
  Spanish, Italian, Portuguese and Russian Lives of Saint Alexis, several Ethiopian and
  Arabic versions, one in Old Norse, one in Georgian, etc.), is incontestable. See my
  article entitled »Les Origines de la Légende de saint Alexis,« which will appear soon
  in *Revue belge de Philologie et d'Histoire.*
3 See my articles "Relationship of the Paris MS. (Bibl. nat., fr. 2162) of the *Vie de saint
  Alexis* to its Latin Source", and "The Humanity of Saint Alexis in the Separation
  Scene of the 13th century Old French Poem (Paris MS. 2162, Bibl. nat.) of the *Vie de
  saint Alexis," Revue belge de Philologie et d'Histoire*, XLIX (1971), No. 3, 862-865.

recueil intitulé le Tombel de Chartrose, Lund, 1946 (*Acta Reg. Societatis Humaniorum litterarum Lundensis*, XLII), pp. 77-105[4]. MS. 244 has also been published in extracts (vv. 74-81, 102-106, 116-117, 164-166, 179-184) by the Abbey Desroches in *Extraits de plusieurs petits poèmes écrits à la fin du XIVe siècle par un prieur du Mont-Saint-Michel.* (Caen, 1837), pp. 372-373. These extracts of some of the pious stories which comprise *Le Tombel de Chartrouse* (manuscript of the fourteenth century, on vellum, containing 84 folios, with initial letters in color) were added by the Abbey Desroches, Jean Jacques, to his *Histoire du Mont-Saint-Michel.*

The anonymous author[5] of our poem (contained in *Le Tombel de Chartrouse*) dedicates this collection of 31 pious stories to the prior and religious of the order of Saint Bruno or *des Chartreux*, apparently with some kind of cenotaphic intention, as revealed in the preamble or dedication of both manuscripts (q.v., below). Our poet, desirous of being buried at this monastery entitled »Fontaine Nostre Dame«[6] although for some unspecified reason not certain of the materialization of his dream, offered to this monastic congregation this pious literary work with the hope of bettering his chances[7].

The dedication of MS. 6835 begins thus:

```
A ses tres chiers seigneurs et peres,
Le prieur Eustache et les freres
De la Fontaigne Notre Dame,
Ung chatif recommande s'ame              4
Qui a despendu longuement
Les besans Dieu trop folement;
Et pour ce qu'il se sent coulpable
Envers la magesté pardurable,           8
Tant qu'il ne pourroit a voir dire
Par soy a l'amende suffire,
Si vous supplie en charité
Que vous par vostre humilité           12
Du relief de vos oraisons
Daignés a ses chativoisons
Faire medicines et secours,
Ains que la mort, qui vient le cours,  16
Du tout en sa prison le tiengne.
Et pour ce qu'il vous en souviengne,
Cest petit livre vous presente;
```

---

4 This edition is, however, not readily available, particularly in the United States.

5 A superficial glance at our text suffices to reveal that our author was undoubtedly a cleric. His good knowledge of the Bible is evident as well as his familiarity with certain church fathers and various religious and historical figures. (See Notes and the Table of Proper Names.)

6 Later better known as Bourg-Fontaine, today part of the commune of Pisseleux, canton of Villers-Cotterêts, department of Aisne.

7 It is a well known fact that the faithful throughout the Middle Ages aspired to be interred in a monasterial church in order to reap its great spiritual fruits.

Et Dieu par sa pitié consente   20
Qu'en tel grace le recuillez
Qu'en vos oraisons l'accueillez
Avecques les autres trespassez.

Our author composed his work in the year 1330 as he states himself in the last
lines of manuscript 244: La veille saint Lorens l'an mil trois cens et trente/ Fu
cest chant translaté s'il est qui s'en demente.
At the priory of Mont-Dol, a prior of Mont-Saint-Michel, named Nicolas
Delauney, finished transcribing the entire work on February 23, 1400, and
this is the aforementioned MS. of Avranches that we now possess at the Bibl.
nat. A note at the end of the MS. attests this transcription:

Scriptum in villa Dolensi anno Domini M°. IIIJ^{co}
vicesimo tercio mense februarii.
Lectores cari curetis queso precari
Pro scriptore Deum salvet ut ille reum.
Per me fratrem Nicholum Delauney prior de Monte Dolis.

In establishing the text, I have remained faithful to the orthography and morphology of the 14th century manuscript. Sporadic emendations have been
made only to render a verse intelligible and all additions placed in brackets are
either obvious emendations or taken from the variant MS. The second table
at the foot of the page contains rejected readings from the base MS.
Modern punctuation and capitalization have been introduced and I have followed in general the recommendations of the committee of the *Société des
anciens textes français*[8] in the use of accents, diereses, distinction of the
vocalic and the consonantal *i* and *j, u* and *v*, numbering of lines, and indication
of the beginning of the columns of each folio of the MS. All abbreviations
have been solved in accordance with those instances where the same words
occur in their full form. Roman numerals have also been uniformly transcribed
in letter form.

1. Versification of MS. 244

The text of MS. 244 contains 992 verses composed of 496 octosyllabic rhymed
couplets. The metrical pattern consists of 304 feminine rhymed couplets and
192 masculine rhymed couplets. The most common masculine rhyme schemes
are: *-ent* (31 couplets), *-é* (27), *-a* (18), *-ez* (12), *-ion* (11), *-ant* (8), *-er* (8),
-ier (7), *-on* (7), and *-eü* (5). There is no example in our poem of 4 consecutive
verses terminating in the same rhyme scheme.

---

8 See *Romania*, 52 (1926), pp. 244-249.

The great predilection of our poet for the rimes riches is attested by his almost impeccable use of the »rimes léonines«. A superficial glance at our poem should suffice to confirm this fact: honour:deshonour 49:50; endroit:orendroit 63:64; ameres:meres 853:854; etc. The same is true for the proper names: Raagaiz:agaiz 701:702; demouré:Honnouré 747:748; verité:Cité 923:924; etc.

Our poet sporadically errs in the matter of syllable-count as exhibited by the following verses: Mais cil mie ne [1a] li lessa 780; Dis [et] set ans touz pleins fournie 587; Dis [et] set ans en penitance 699; etc.

The abundant use of enjambements throughout the poem is most evident and does not require, in my opinion, any textual references.

Note, in particular, the rhymes mouvray 553 (fut. 1 of *movoir*): recouvray 554 (past part. of *recovrer*); pechëors:emperëours 801:802; and merite:escript 927:928. (See Phonology, below.)

It is apparent that in spite of our poet's strict compliance with the »léonines« rhyme schemes which had to necessitate considerable research and tax his poetic resources and versatility, the poem reads very well. We must therefore conclude that our author was a gifted versifier, able to manipulate a difficult metrical pattern and create a simple, easy-flowing, and agreable style.

2. Language of MS. 244

In our text, polysyllables ending in an atonic *e* are consistently elided before a word beginning with a vowel: Saint Pol nos enseigne et declaire 1; Et lor habondance en poverte 25; De lettreüre en mielx s'adresce 142; etc. Only a few sporadic variations occur: Cil mette entre nos tel [a]corde 366 (The insertion of initial *a* avoids the hiatus); Au di[e]menche, apres les messes 582 (The replacement of the MS. form *dimenche* by the more regular OF form *dïemenche* easily eliminates the hiatus.); also Un jour de di[e]menche oroient 716. With regard to monosyllables whose elision is usually optional, several examples of hiatus are present in our poem: Ne en rien il ne se delite 239; En assemblees ne en presses 581; Que entretant n'avoit pris garde 821; Ne unquez le prix d'une maille 918; etc.

Enclitic forms are practically nonexistent in our text except for enclisis of the personal pronoun *le* (masculine and neuter) which appears quite frequently after *ne*: Nel fist pas a oiseuse entendre 125; Chacun le quert, mes nul nel treuve 435; Tout soit ce qu'ilz nel voient mie 518; Quar ja en cel point nel veïssent 580; Son pere qui nel cognut mie 648; En ton hostel, et nel me change 654; Tout nel voulist le seignor mie 679; but *ne le* in verses 610, 672, 765, etc.

I found no examples of enclisis of the definite article in the masculine singular after *en*: en l'encloistre 451; En l'epistre 508; En l'ostel 639; en l'ostel 675; etc.

However, *ou*, variant of *el* (=en le), occurs sporadically in our poem: ou travail 722; ou champ 917; Ou quint livre de la Cité 924; etc. In the plural, we invariably find *es*: es grans tormens 27; es roiaulx thronez 32; es coupx 97; es cieulx 525; etc.

3. Phonology

Vowels

A Both tonic and atonic a + i̯ (yod) generally diphthongize to *ai*: faire 152, 506, 547, etc.; laisser 514; repaire 561, 958, 978, etc.; haire 739 (Frankish *hâr ja > VL hari̯a > haire); traire 810; etc.; but the *ai* diphthong frequently monophthongizes to open *e* (ę) as attested by the rhymes *nestre* (nascere): *estre* (essere) 339:340 and *lermes* (lacrimas):*termes* (terminos) 533:534; also lermes 415, 533, 864; lessast 465 (laxavisset); bessa:lessa 779:780; lermoïer 847; lessé 951; delessance 989; etc.

The *ai* diphthong also occurs as *ei/ey*: repeire 253, 767; pleinte 691; scey (sapio > sa(p)i̯o) 760; and as *oi*: soi 293, 427, 429; etc.

In the 1st person singular of the future, *ai/ay* is sporadically assimilated to é (< Latin á) as attested by the rhyme *mouvray* (future 1 of *movoir*): *recouvray* (past past. of *recovrer*) 553:554.

Accented *a* followed by a nasal (and sporadically by palatalized *n* < ni̯, gn) > *ain*, with only sporadic deviations: vaine 625; main 776, 787; saine 887; etc.; but Chalemeine (Carolum + magnum) 182; meinge 367 (maneat). Note that tonic close *e* before a nasal usually occurs as *ai*: paine (pena): plaine (plena) 419:420; paine 834 (pena); plaine (plena) 888; etc.

Ain and *ein* are identical in sound as attested by the rhymes ameine:Chalemeine 181:182; mains (manos):mains (minus) 195:196 and 243:244; creindre:maindre 309:310; and saine (sana):plaine (plena) 887:888.

The distinction between *an* and *en* is rigorously maintained. The words *grant* 42, 214, 289, etc.; *sans* 115, 224, 225, 225, etc.; *enfant* 194, 555, 857, etc.; always appear with *an*. The forms *temps* 17, 74, 264, 341, etc.; dolens 563; ceens 793, 830; invariably occur with *en*. No rhyme *an:en* is found in our text. See the popular *-ant* rhyme scheme which attests this distinction: 603:604; 765:766; 769:770; etc.[1].

Note, however, the form *fame* 102, 285 (femina) along with the more common form *femme* 208, 504, 836, etc.

The common Latin suffix *-ator* occurs as *-iere* in the analogical form *emperiere* 78 (even though the free accented *a* is not preceded by a palatal) and rhymes with *planiere* (*plenariam) 77.

---

1 Cf. the 13th century version (MS. 2162) of the *Vie de saint Alexis* where en and an are identical in sound as attested by the rhyme *entent:garant* 213:214.

E (close). Tonic free close e (ę) regularly diphthongizes to *oi*: voie 72, 344; soie 82, 83; quoi 127, 829; avoir 248; doit 505, 509; soi 528; croire 529; etc. Few vestiges of the earlier *ei* diphthong are recorded except for *meins*(minus) 134, 148. Note also *hers* 115 for *heirs*(*herem) and *beire* 768(Frankish *bera) rhyming with *repeire* 767. The more common form *biere* occurs in verses 828, 867, and the rhyme biere:maniere 879:880 seems to clearly attest that it was pronounced -ęre.

As noted above, accented close *e* before a nasal usually occurs as *-ain*: paines 852; paine 834; etc.

E (open). Open *e* usually shows regular phonetic development. Tonic open e (ę) regularly > *ie*: convient 6; bien 9, 54, 833, etc.; viens 69; etc.; but grefs 43 (grěves); quert 435 (quěrit).

Accented open *e* + yod > *i*: despit 19 (despéctum); respit 20; lit 370, 547, 553; etc. Note the correct phonetic form cimetire 600 (Eccl. Latin coemetérium) rhyming with dire 599.

I (close). Tonic or pretonic close *i* exhibits normal phonetic development.

O (close). Unaccented close *o* (free or checked) > *ou/o* [u], with the former predominating:recouvree 316; honouré:descoulouré 629:630; aouree:ajournee 735:736; ourant:courant 765:766; souffrir 832; etc.; but redoter 439; dolosoit 550; orant:plorant 603:604; etc.

Unaccented open *o* (free or checked) also > *ou/o* [u], with the former predominating: demourez 307, 722; trouva 375; descoulouré 630; demouré 698, 747; retourna 782; demourassent 941; etc.; but demoroit 566; retorna 631; retorner 646; retornerent 785; etc. Note *turterelle* 560 (VL turturella).

Tonic free close *o* > *ou/o*, with the former predominating and rarely > *eu*: honour:deshonour 49:50; honnour 73; mours 102, 194, 204, etc.; flour 202, 437; dolour 253, 420; amour 463; emperëours 802, 866; odour 886; etc.; but amor 107, 664; honnor 233; greignor 275, 490, 548; jor 403; pechëors 801; adjutore:victore 911:912; etc.; and seuffrent 3; honneur 175; doleurs 268; seul 981; etc.

Ou and *o* [u] < tonic close *o* are identical in sound as attested by the rhyme pechëors:emperëours 801:802.

O (open). Tonic free open *o* > *ue*, which usually > *eu*: cuer 227, 242, 258, etc.; suer 300, 330, etc.; but treuve 228, 435; peut 235, 246, 259, etc.; veult 245, 482, 496, etc.; preuve 436; seur 504; deul 543; etc. Note, in particular, the form *neuces* 212, 221, 250, etc. (VL *nŏptias, for CL nuptias) instead of the more common OF form *noces*. The palatal combination pti which normally checks a preceding vowel has invariably failed to do so in our text with regard to this word where tonic open *o* (ǫ) always diphthongizes to *eu*.

U (close). Tonic and pretonic close *u* exhibit normal phonetic development.

92

Consonants

C Initial *c* + *a* > *ch*: change 203; chiere 300; chartre 772, 779, 787, etc.
C pronounced as [ts] and consonantal combinations with yod pronounced [ts] are generally written *c*: Sapience:pacïence 67:68; conscïence:reverence 235:236; excellence:innocence 323:324; etc.; but quite frequently as *sc*, perhaps a transitional stage from *ts* to *s*[2]: noblesce:adresce 141:142; adresce:leesce 227:228; richesce:destresce 951:952; etc.

Dentals (d, t)

Intervocalic *d* or *t* is consistently lost except for a considerable number of learned and semi-learned words: mué 22; vie:oÿe 111:112; fiance 901; etc.; but paradis 73; verité 445, 923, etc.; adjutore 911; etc. Note, however, *odit* 575 (audivit).

Final dental, if loose (id est, unsupported by a consonant or the product of assimilation) is lost: mué 22; onnesté:esté 113:114; dure 224; etc. Final *t* is generally lost in the preterite tense: Alexi:essi 117:118; fu 218, 296, 432, 462, etc.; parti:parti 543:544; Alexi:texi 985:986; etc.; but fut 202, 276, 403, etc.; odit (preterite 3 of oïr) 575; and jut 884.

Final dentals, if loose, had disappeared from the pronunciation even if they were retained in the orthography[3].

G Note that the form *poi* (paucum) 131, 253, 263, 543, 944, always occurs in our text, never *peu*. In this paroxytone, the final *g* has undoubtedly gone to yod[4]. (Cf. pai < paco.)

L The *l* in *vi[l]té* (cité:vi[l]té 609:610) is, of course, not pronounced and explains why the scribe wrote *vité*. I could just as well have left it thus.

Nasals (m and n)

No confusion whatsoever occurs between final *m* and *n* after a vowel.

Except for *nom* (nomen) 76, 117, 389, etc.; final *m* has consistently been reduced to *n*.

Note that *m* has been partially denasalized to *p* in *dampnez* 51 (damnatos). This partial denasalization sometimes occurs in the pronunciation of Latin and early learned loan-words such as *damner* and *damnedeu*[5]. Cf. Old Provencal domna/dompna.

Note that although spelled *gn*, the nasal is not palatalized in *assigna*(:disna) 667:668. The same holds true for Chalemeine (-magnum) 182 rhyming with *ameine* 181.

After *r*, final *n* is invariably lost: jour:sejour 549:550; etc.

---

2 See A. Stimming, *Der anglonormannische Boeve de Hauntone* (Halle, 1899), p. 232.
3 Cf. the 13th century OF version (MS. 2162) where the following rhymes bear this out: gari:David 454:455; vreté:contét 847:848; and apelé:sonét 851:852.
4 See Kr. Nyrop, *Grammaire historique de la langue française* (Gyldendal, 1967), # 417,1.
5 M. K. Pope, *From Latin to Modern French with especial consideration of Anglo-Norman* (Manchester-England, 1952), # 369.

Labials

Labials exhibit normal phonetic development and necessitate few remarks except for the following:

Note the retention of labials in the following words: grefs 43; escripture: desconfiture 153:154; route:doubte 707:708; doubte:toute 723:724; merite:escript 927:928. It is obvious from the above rhyme schemes that these unassimilated labials were not pronounced.

S Etymological *s* has religiously been retained before consonants including *m* and *n*: despit 19; desclaire 66, 957, 962; meslee 97; pasma:blasma 819:820; but declaire l. The rhymes septime:abisme 379:380 and assigna: disna 667:668 clearly attest the fact that this *s*, although it was retained in the orthography, was not pronounced by our scribe.

4. Morphology

The Definite Article
The only form of *li* (nom. pl.) recorded in our text occurs in *li plusieurs* (feminine) 412 and *li plusieurs* (masculine) 739.

Substantive and Adjective
In our 14th century text, the Old French two case inflectional system which remained practically intact until well into the thirteenth century (excluding the Anglo-Norman dialect)[1] is rendered conspicuous by its almost complete absence[2]. The nominative singular of both masculine substantives and adjectives religiously occurs without the inflectional -*s*: Quant le cler jor fut ajorné 403; Le saint Livre de Sapience 67 (subject of *desclaire* 66); Unques plus d'eulx nul fruit n'essi 118; festoié 643 (nom. sing.); salué 643 (nom. sing.); Dont il est né 795; etc. The nominative plural of both masculine nouns and adjectives consistently ends in -*s*: Quar se noz parens sunt loiaux 515; les Rommains (nom. pl.) 185, 708, 912; Grans et petiz a Dieu oroient 737; Les sains 275; etc.

There exists, however, some apparent confusion in our poem with regard to the inflection of substantives and adjectives derived from imparisyllabic Latin nouns originally of the 3rd classical declension: Comme se ce fust un *emperiere* 78 (imperator); but Lors dist *l'emperëour* Archade 800 (imperatorem). Note that our poet uses the nominative singular form *mendre* 489 (menor) instead

---

1 See P. Studer's edition of *Le Mystère d'Adam* (Manchester, 1962), p. xlviii.
2 Cf. the 13th century version (MS. *O*) where, in general, the two case inflectional system is rigorously maintained. See, for example, laisse XXVIII of my edition (*Romania*, tome 92, 1971, pages 1-36) whose rhyme scheme religiously observes the distinction. See, in addition, laisses IX, XII, XXX, etc., of MS. 2162 of the 13th century version.

of the correct accusative form *menor/menour* (prendre le bien mendre por delaisser le greignor). *Greignor* (oblique case, from grandiorem) also appears in verses 275, 334, etc.

The etymologically proper OF nominative singular form *feu* (=OF *fel*) occurs in verse 701 while the OF nominative singular form *seur* (soror) appears in verse 504 as an accusative singular in place of *serour* (sororem).

The feminine of 2nd class adjectives (id est, those declined like the nouns of the classical 3rd declension and whose masculine and feminine forms were identical: *qualis, grandis, mortalis, fortis,* etc.) occurs with or without analogical -*e* according to the needs of the meter and rhyme. The etymologically correct phonetic forms, however, appear much more frequently: grant multitude 137; grans pompes 213; grant melodie 217; ceste mortel vie 229; ceste mortel region 331; tel [a]corde 366; quel cause 427; charnel affection 472 (Eccl. Latin carnalem); charnel appartenance 513; quel terre 795; quel chartre 816; etc. A few examples of analogical -*e* are sporadically recorded: malvestié grande et amere 462; celle gent ville (vilem) et orde 714; ville 954; forte chose 950 (fortem).

Note *doloreux* voie 231 but elsewhere the feminine form of the adjecitve invariably occurs: la voie plus excellente et plus preste 247:248; etc.; toutes les *nouvealx* mariees 418 (See Notes.), and the feminine superlative form *santiesme* succession 86 derived from the classical *sanctissimam.*

Demonstratives (adjective and pronoun)
Even greater inflectional confusion is evident with respect to the demonstrative adjectives and pronouns. In the nominative singular (masculine), we usually find the correct OF form *cil* (VL *celli, by analogy with *qui,* for *ecce ille*). See, for example, verses 191 (adj.), 804 (adj.), 221 (pron.), 327 (pron.), 356 (pron.); etc. However, *celli* occurs frequently as subject (verses 278, 425, 502, 596, 970, 978). Sporadically, the oblique form *cel* appears in the nominative case (verses 129, 252); also *cestui* 98; *cest* 141. In the oblique singular (masculine), the common OF forms *cel* (22, 74, 115, 121, etc.; *icel* 744) and *cest* (231, 255, 304, etc.) are generally recorded. Note, however, *cil* 589 and *celi* 751.

Personal Pronouns
The personal pronouns give occasion for the following remarks:
The masculine nominative plural *il* is found with or without the -*s*[3] (*z* in our text): il firent 39; il sentiront 43; il orent 114; il touchassent 879; etc.; but ilz se verront 36; ilz repaissoient 106; Ilz vesquirent 120; Ilz li eüssent 470; etc.

---

3 The -*s* was added towards the end of the 13th century. See Schwan-Behrens, *Grammaire de l'ancien français,* trad. O. Bloch (Leipzig, 1923), # 322, 3.

Although no example is found in our poem of the masculine plural forms *il/ils/ilz* replacing the feminine form *eles*, a trait characteristic of the West or North[4], one does occur in verse 30 of the Prologue.

El, the monosyllabic western form[5] of the feminine personal pronoun *ele/elle*, consistently occurs in our text: el estoit 410; el respondit 419; el est 595 (=son oraison); el 615 (=sa conscïence); el faisoit 864; el doit estre 928. I found only one example of *elle*: Qu'elle ne lor pot nul mot dire 411.

The oblique case (cas régime) of the tonic masculine personal pronoun invariably appears as *li*: De li 97, 445, 502, 559, etc.; par devers li 287; por li 340, 563; o li 401; en li 463, 593; avec li 900, 992. In the 13th century and especially in the 14th, atonic *li* was confused with tonic *lui* and frequently employed as the accented form[6]. This use of atonic *li* for tonic *lui* was especially common in the West[7]. Note, in addition, *a lié* (=à elle) 294.

Li (sing.) and *lor/lour* (plur.) invariably occur as the atonic dative forms for both genders: Si li est grant desconfiture 154 (masc.); se Dieu li envoie 232 (masc.); li a presté 241 (masc.); il li sermonna 355 (fem.); li donna 356 (fem.); Et li dist 360 (fem.); etc.; lor donna 116 (masc.); lour envoia 121 (masc.); ne lor pot nul mot dire 411 (fem.); etc.

Possessives

The atonic feminine forms of the possessive adjectives *ma, ta,* and *sa,* are consistently elided before vowels: s'esperance 238; s'espouse 292; m'amie 300; s'ame 482. The modern use of the masculine singular forms *mon, ton,* and *son,* before feminine nouns beginning with a vowel appears only once in our text: Son oraison est si eslite 594.

This modern use dates all the way back to the end of the 12th century in the dialects of Old Lorraine and Old Walloon. It appears later in the other OF dialects and its use does not become consistent in other dialects until later Middle French (14th century in Francien)[8].

Verbs. Present Indicative

Our text employs only forms with the analogical *-e* in the first person singular of *-er* verbs: j'espoire 88; ameine 181; je regarde 822; je recorde 934; etc. Therefore, the 1st person singular is invariably undifferentiated from the 3rd person singular[9]. In Anglo-Norman, analogical forms in *-e* begin to appear as

---

4 See Pope, # 1251.

5 Ibid.

6 See Nyrop, # 528, 4.

7 See Lucien Foulet, *Petite Syntaxe de l'ancien français* (Paris, 1965), p. 364 ff.

8 See Nyrop, # 547, and Pope, # 860.

9 Cf. MS. 2162 of the 13th century version where only forms without the analogical *-e* are recorded resulting in an invariable differentiation between the 1st person singular and the 3rd person singular: *pens* 135 / *pense* 128; *desir* 1082 / *desire* 348, 962; etc.

early as the 12th century, were quite common in the 2nd half of the 13th century, and became dominant in the second half of the 14th century[10]. Though analogical -*s* begins to appear sporadically in the 13th century in the 1st person singular of OF -*re* and -*ir* (non-inchoative) type verbs, its use is not generalized until the close of the Middle Ages (15th century)[11]. Only forms without -*s* occur in our text: requier 306; vien 764; sui 420; suy 424; etc. With the exceptions of *sommes* 50, 620, 802, and *servons* 345 (imperative), only the -*on* forms are recorded in the first person plural of the present indicative and imperative for all conjugations: avon 56; voulon 336, 621; devon 809, 965; ensivon 343 (imperative). The use of the termination -*on* is characteristic of the western region and seems to be an endeavor to limit -*s* to the second person. The termination -*on* does occur in Francien but its use disappears in the 15th century[12]. Cf. the Old Provencal endings for the 1st person plural (-*am, em: amam, amem*).

If I am not mistaken, only the -*on* forms occur in the future indicative: aron 334; porron 335; pourron 346; saron 809; diron 969. Likewise, only the -*ion* forms appear in the imperfect indicative and conditional: voulion 332; estion 337; savion 799; perdrion 333. The use of the ending -*ion* in the 1st person plural of the imperfect indicative and conditional is also characteristic of the western region[13].

In the imperfect indicative and conditional, our 14th century text invariably employs the -*oie, -oies, -oit,* etc., endings. The -*oie* termination replaced the -*eie* ending in the 12th century[14]. The final -*e* in the 1st person singular was generally not pronounced in our poem (the ending -*oie* thus being monosyllabic) as attested by the following verses: Que celli qu'espousé avoie,/ Que plus que rien du monde amoie 425:426; Mon doulx enfant que tant amoie/ Qui estoit ma vie et ma joie 555:556; Du bien que de toi attendoie./ James ou monde n'avray joie 825:826; etc. Although originally syllabic in early Old French, the final -*e* became mute very early and in several texts was not even retained in orthography[15]. Whether the termination -*oie* is monosyllabic or disyllabic in our poem depends on the needs of the meter and rhyme. The same is true for the final -*e* in the second person singular (-*oies*) as attested by the following verses: Que tu nostre cher filz estoies? / Certes, pas souffrir ne devoies,/ 831:832; Ne demonstrer qui tu estoies,/ Mes de tes serjans enduroies 849:850; etc.; but -*oies* is disyllabic in verse 846: Tu nos vëoies en dement; etc.

I believe that only one etymological form survives in our text: ert 644 (erat) although they lived on into the 14th century[16]. The analogical form *estoie* consistently replaces *ere/iere:* estoit 87, 88, 100, 104, etc.; estoient 401; etc.

---

10 See Schwan-Behrens, # 352, and Pope, # 898.
11 Schwan-Behrens, # 374, and # 363.   14 Schwan-Behrens, # 365.
12 Pope, # 894, and p. 503, # xv.   15 Nyrop, # 161.
13 Pope, p. 503, # xv.   16 Pope, # 920.

Moreover, the popular etymological synthetic future forms of *estre*: ier, iers, iert, etc. (ero, etc.) are not recorded in our text[17].

In the first conjugation future stems, note that in *retourra* 18 (:corra) the unaccented intertonic vowel *a* is effaced between *n-r*, both of which then assimilate to *rr*. However, the intertonic *a* between *r-r* becomes *e* in *dureront* 260. In the atypical form *demeinray* 552 (de + VL minare), the intertonic *a* is lost but the secondary consonant group *n'r* does not assimilate to *rr*.

In the 1st person plural of the preterite, we find by analogy (analogy most often purely orthographic) with the 2nd person plural whose *s* before *t* was effaced in the 13th century[18], the forms redoubtasmes:trouvasmes 59:60. Needless to say, this analogical *s* is not pronounced. Elsewhere, only forms without this orthographic *s* occur: despisimes:veïmes 45:46. Note, in addition, the analogical form mourirent 916 (:combatirent 915).

The following infinitive forms frequently appear in the West: voier:soier 393:394; and pourvoier:voier 757:758[19].

Present Subjunctive

The analogical *-e* is sporadically recorded in the present subjunctive of the 1st conjugation: je repaire 360 (Low Latin repatriem). Cf. repaire 561, 958 (pres. ind., < repatriat). The etymological forms, however, consistently occur in our poem: envoit 661 (pres. subj.); but envoie 232 (pres. ind.); remaint 675 (pres. ind.); etc.

The infix -ge [dze] was employed in West French and was adopted from verbs such as *tergam* where the form was the regular development of the radical[20]. Several examples appear in our text: apprenge 163; meinge 367; tienge 954. Unfortunately, these forms were also used in the southern region[21]. They are not, therefore, proper to the west region and cannot serve (by themselves) to localize our text.

Note the analogical form *truisse* 765 (pres. subj. 1 of *trover*) perhaps by analogy with such verbs as *puisse* 316 (VL *possiat or Gallo-Latin *poscat)[22].

For the *-on* termination in *soion* 801, see present indicative, above.

Imperative

A conscious attempt has been made to derive the 2nd person singular imperative form directly from the classical form or its reconstructed VL form (in all conjugations): ayes 68 (habeas); met 590 (mitte); fay 652, 655 (fac); change 654 (cambia).

17 Cf. the 13th century version: *iert* 71, 273, 274, etc. (*erit*).
18 Schwan-Behrens, # 355; cf. # 342.
19 Pope, p. 503, # xviii; cf. # 963.
20 Pope, p. 503, # xvii, and especially # 910.
21 Ibid.
22 Schwan-Behrens, # 348, 4, and # 361, 2.

Vocalic Alternation

The differences effected by vocalic alternation are consistently maintained in our text (See Phonology) though a tendency to regularize the conjugated forms is sporadically discernible, e.g., *je vos en proie* (preco) 343 instead of the correct phonetic form *pri*, to render the stem of this form identical to the other conjugated forms which appear in our text: proier 297, 711 (correct phonetic form, from *precare*); proiere 299 (correct phonetic form, from Merovingian Latin *precariam*); but priere 116, 990; and prier 874. Cf. *Roland*: priet and preir, leier, otreir (correct phonetic form) with their doublets prier, liier, otriier[23].

5. Conclusion

Perhaps the most salient trait of our poet (and/or scribe) is his consistency, consistency as a versifier (see various rhyme schemes; his use of elision, enclisis; etc.); consistency with respect to the phonology and orthography (e.g.: rigorous distinction between *an* and *en*; regular diphthongization of tonic free close *e* to *oi*; accented free close *o* > *ou/o*, and rarely > *eu*; tonic free open *o* usually > *eu*; lack of alternative orthographic forms as attested, for example, by the spelling of the final nasal consonant; religious retention of etymological *s* before consonants including *m* and *n*; etc.). The same consistency is manifested in the morphology (the conspicuous absence of the Old French two case inflectional system; the predilection of our poet, in general, for etymologically correct phonetic forms with regard to the feminine of 2nd class adjectives; the use of monosyllabic *el*; of *li* and *lor/lour*; the elision of the atonic feminine forms of the possessive adjective before vowels; the invariable presence of analogical *-e* in the first person singular of *-er* verbs; the *-on* forms recorded in the 1st person plural of the present indicative and future, as well as *-ion* in the imperfect indicative and conditional; the invariable use of the *-oie*, etc., terminations in the imperfect indicative and conditional; the predilection of our author for the etymologically correct phonetic forms in the present subjunctive and imperative, as well as his general retention of the differences effected by vocalic alternation; etc.). Needless to say, this characteristic of our poet (coupled, of course, with his artistic skill) contributed considerably to the readability and easy-flowingness of our text.

It is clear that our anonymous author, undoubtedly a cleric (See Introduction.), uses, in general, the literary language of his time. It is equally apparent that although our text shows a mixture of dialectal features, the preponderance of western characteristics is obvious and sufficient linguistic diagnostic traits

---

23 Cf. MS. 2162: *proie* (VL precat) 123, 200, 378, etc.; and *proient* 733, 1213, for *prient*.

occur to conclude that our text belongs to the western region of France, perhaps to the northwest, towards Normandy. A superficial glance at the linguistic section (phonology and especially the morphology) should suffice to confirm this fact (e.g.: the diphthong $ai > ę$; the early disintegration of the 2 case inflectional system[24]; the use of *el*, the monosyllabic western form of the feminine personal pronoun; the use of atonic *li* for tonic *lui*; the termination *-on/-ion* in the verb system; the infinitive forms *voier, soier,* etc.; the infix *-ge* in the present subjunctive; etc.).

Likewise, the evidence gathered in the section on phonology and morphology suffices to date our base MS. from the 1st half ot the 14th century, 1330 being the date given by our author in the last lines of MS. 244. (See Introduction.)

---

24 Pope, p. 502, # xii.

De Saint Alexi qui fut dis set ans chiex son pere come povre [72a]

     Saint Pol nos enseigne et declaire
     Que celx qui veulent a Dieu plaire
     Seuffrent touz persequcions,
4   Et que par tribulacions
     Que les bons ont a soustenir,
     Convient au regne Dieu venir.
     Et Prosper dit en verité
8   Que c'est droite necessité
     Que les malvés, qui nul bien n'aiment, [72b]
     Les despisent au monde et claiment
     Por folx chaistiz et hors de sens,
12   Quar ilz perdent les biens presens
     Ou de rien lor cure ne mettent,
     Et en lieu de ce se promettent
     Les grans biens du ciel pardurables
16   Qui ne sunt pas ici voiables.
     Mais gueres de temps ne corra
     Que le vroi juge retourra
     Sur les despisans son despit,
20   Quant la mort, dont il n'ont respit,
     Malgré lour touz coiz les fera.
     Lors a cel point mué sera
     Par tresdigne conversion
24   Lour orguil en confusion
     Et lor habondance en poverte,
     Quar ilz seront par leur desserte
     Es grans tormens d'enfer jetez,
28   Et celx qui ci furent betez
     Et traictiez deshonnestement,
     Qui endurerent humblement

---

10 clamet

Lors cruaultez et lors ramponez,
32 Seront assis es roiaulx thronez
Et avec Dieu les jugeront.
Adonc les orgueilleux seront
Horriblement espoëntez
36 Quant ilz se verront tormentez
Sans nul espoir d'allegement,
Et celx regner si noblement
A qui il firent maint oultrage.
40 Ja por avoir ne por parage
Ne trouveront qui les cognoisse.   [72c]
Lors gemiront par grant angoisse
Es grefs tormens qu'il sentiront
44 Et par esmay entr'elx diront:
»Vez ci celx que nos despisimes
Quant ou monde bas les veïmes;
Entre nos foulx toute lor vie
48 Repution par desverie
Et que lor fin fust sans honour.
Or sommes nos a deshonour
Dampnez en nostre iniquité,
52 Et eulx par lour benignité
Sunt entre les filz Dieu comptez.
Bien sunt de bas en hault montez
Et nos de hault en bas cheüz.
56 Les biens que nos avon eüz
S'en sunt plus tost qu'oisel volez.
Trop fumes au monde affolez
Qui les malx point ne redoubtasmes
60 Qu'apres la mort tantost trouvasmes.«
     Telx complains diront en enfer
Et seront mielx lïez qu'en fer
Les malvés qui en maint endroit
64 Es servans Dieu font orendroit
Assez d'ennuy et de maltraire,
Si come moult bel le desclaire
Le saint Livre de Sapience.
68 Ayes donc bonne pacïence,

---

35 espoventes
45 Ve
57 que o.

Tu qui viens au divin servise,
Et ne te chault en nulle guise
Se tu es ci mis au derriere,
72   Quar c'est la voie et la maniere
D'avoir honnour en paradis.   [72d]
     Il ot en cel temps de jadis
A Romme un noble crestïen
76   Qui ot a nom Eufemïen.
Et tenoit cort aussi planiere
Com se ce fust un emperiere;
Quar trois mille hommes le servoient
80   Qui par mi ses palais alloient,
Comme filz de contes parez
De seins de soie et d'or barrez
Et vestuz de robes de soie.
84   Si ne vivoit il pas de proie
Mais de loial possession,
Santiesme succession.
Et n'estoit pas par vaine gloire,
88   Ains estoit, si comme j'espoire,
Por les ennemis de l'empire
Espoventer et desconfire;
Que guerre es Rommains ne presissent
92   Ceulx qui si puissans les veïssent,
Quar si comme nous sentencie
Le Livre de Chevalerie:
Nul n'ose commencer bataille
96   O cil qu'il entent que mielx vaille
De li es coupx de la meslee.
Por ce faisoit cestui monstree
De sa force et de sa richesce,
100   Quar il estoit en sa haultesce
Misericors et piteable.
Et fame a ses mours raisonable,
De hault lieu, avoit espousee,
104   Qui Aglaes estoit appellee.
Touz les jours trois tables tenoient   [73a]
De povre gent qu'ilz repaissoient
Por l'amor de Dieu purement,

---

74 cil
78 feust
97 D. lui e.

103

108	Et les servoit moult noblement	
	Il meïsmes en sa personne.	
	Et le son disner apres nonne	
	Prenoit o gens de saincte vie	
112	Ne ja n'y fust parole oÿe	
	Fors de salu et d'onnesté.	
	Quant il orent grant piece esté	
	Sans avoir hers en cel maniere,	
116	Dieu lor donna a lour priere	
	Un filz qui ot nom Alexi.	
	Unquez plus d'eulx nul fruit n'essi,	
	Quar par commun assentement	
120	Ilz vesquirent puis chastement	
	Que Dieu cel filz lour envoia,	
	Qui a Dieu amer s'avoia,	
	Des ce qu'il ot entendement.	
124	Et son bon pere vroiement	
	Nel fist pas a oiseuse entendre,	
	Mais li fist des set ans apprendre	
	De quoi touz les nobles savoient	
128	A cel temps et mielx en valoient.	
	Or est failli cel bon usage.	
	Princes et gens de hault parage	
	Font mes poi lors enfans apprendre;	
132	La gent fauvel lor font entendre:	
	Se de la clergie savoient,	
	Que meins aux armes en vauld[r]oient.	
	Mais a ce ne s'accorde mie	
136	Le Livre de Chevalerie	
	Qui dit bien que grant multitude	[73b]
	Et force sans doctrine et rude	
	Ne vainquent pas si prestement	
140	Com art et exercitement,	
	Et cest art par la grant noblesce	
	De lettreüre en mielx s'adresce	
	Et a sa perfection monte.	
144	Si est a ceulx dommage et honte	
	Qui a garder provinces ont	
	Quant plus lettrez de ceulx ne sont	

----

126 lui

115 avoirs
126 ais a.

104

Qui es champs labourent et fenent.
148 Mains en valent et meins en penent
Celx qui des livres ne sunt sages;
Et entre les autres dommages
Que je ne puis pas touz retraire,
152 Seg[r]etement ne peut rien faire
Prince qui n'entent escripture;
Si li est grant desconfiture,
Meïsmement quant il guerroye,
156 Scïence dont, se Dieu me voye,
Amende et ennoblist proesce
Et li fait par sa subtillesce
En touz lieux avoir excellence.
160 Et si vault mainte faiz scïence
La ou force ne peut atteindre,
Et por ce ne se doit nul feindre
Qu'il n'apprenge de la clergie,
164 Quar scïence o chevalerie
C'est ferme tour sur roche assise,
C'est fine esmeraude en or mise,
Qui fait touz temps ses porsoians
168 Estre riches et cler voians,
Seürs, puissans et allosez.   [73c]
Entre vos, dont, qui proposez
Vivre chevalerousement,
172 Apprenez tout seürement
Des livres, et mieulx en vauldrez,
Ne ja par ce point ne fauldrez
A honneur de chevalerie.
176 Touz les rois sceurent de clergie
Dont les faiz sunt plus en memore,
Et tousjours eurent plus de glore
Celx qui plus amerent scïence.
180 A tesmoing de ceste sentence
Le grant roi Alexandre ameine,
David, Cesar et Chalemeine,
Qui touz de la clergie sceurent
184 Et sur touz glore et poair eurent,
Et les Rommains qui toutes terres

---

154 lui
158 lui
162 d. mie f.

Plus par scïence que par guerres
Mistrent en lor subjectiön.

188 Mais c'est trop grant digression
De ce que proposé avoie,
Si est droiz que je m'y ravoie.
  Cil noble prince Eufemïen

192 Selon le bon us ancïen
Fist apprendre o grant diligence
A son enfant mours et scïence,
Qu'il ne semblast ouvrier de mains.

196 Si ne sot il pas por ce mains
D'armes, de bois, ne de riviere.
N'est rien qui a noble home affiere
Dont bien aider ne se sceüst.

200 N'estoit nul a qui ne pleüst
Sa courtoisie et sa noblesce.
Quant il fut en flour de jeunesce
Qui change neïs es plus sages

204 Souvent en pis mours et corages,
Son pere le voult marïer.
Tout ne l'oïst il escrïer
De rien qui feïst a reprendre.

208 Si li fist une femme prendre,
Belle pucelle, jeune et sage,
Et de l'imperial lignage.
Moult ot a Romme la journee

212 Des neuces grant feste menee
A grans despens et a grans pompes:
Moult y ot grant resson de trompes
Et de tabours et de cimbales;

216 Moult ot en chambres et en sales
Grans deduiz et grant melodie;
Moult fu la feste bien servie
Et tout a point et a plenté.

220 Mais aillors ot sa volenté
Cil por qui les neuces estoient,
Quar touz ses desirers tiroient
A la parfaicte envoiseüre

224 Du ciel, qui sans departir dure

[73d]

---

188 g. addigression   222 desirs
208 lui

217 Suns d.

Et sans ennui et sans moleste.
Qui au desir de ceste feste
Applique son cuer et adresce,
228 Il ne treuve de leesce
Es biens de ceste mortel vie
Ne n'a de nulle chose envie
Qu'en cest secle doloreux voie.
232 Neporquant, se Dieu li envoie
Puissance, honnor ou dignité,   [74a]
O temporel felicité,
Il peut a bonne conscïence
236 L'apoursaër pour reverence
De la divine pourveance.
Mais il n'y met pas s'esperance
Ne en rien il ne se delite,
240 Mais pense comment il s'aquitte
De ce que Dieu li a presté;
Et est son cuer plus tempesté
D'avoir largement entre mains
244 Que s'il eüst a prendre mains,
Quar quicunques veult Dieu ensuivre,
S'il peut et povre et humble vivre,
C'est la voie plus excellente
248 Et plus preste a avoir s'entente.
        Tantdiz come ceulx s'esbatoient
Qui aux neuces venuz estoient,
Le bruman pensa sagement
252 Comment tout cel esbatement
Repeire a dolour et poi dure,
Et comment la garde et la cure
Des biens de cest monde est mordable
256 Et le delit escoulourgeable
Et la glore tantost fenie,
Et quicunques son cuer y lie
Ne peut es vroiz biens avenir
260 Qui dureront sans ja fenir
Lassus en pardurable vie.
Si li sembla que la partie

---

232 lui   252 Comme t.
238 mett p.   259 b. venir
241 lui   262 lui s.
250 au

D'estre ci un poi en mesaise
264 Por estre apres touz temps a e[i]se
Valoit mieulx sans compareison [74b]
Qu'avoir ses bons une saison
Por estre apres en la plenté
268 De toutes doleurs tormenté
Sans fin et sans redemption.
Si prist deliberacion
Que touz biens mondains lesseroit
272 Et au monde povre seroit
Por estre riche en paradis,
Quar ainsi le firent jadis
Les sains dont l'en fait greignor feste.
276 Au soir quant la chambre fut preste
Et d'estranges gens delivree,
Celli qui n'avoit sa pensee
A vanitez ne a frivoles,
280 S'embla assez tost des caroles
Et vint coyement a la chambre
Qui fleroit comme pomme d'ambre,
D'espices et de robes fines.
284 Lors cercha entor les cortines
Qu'il n'y eüst fame ne homme.
Si fist tout vuider, c'est la somme,
Et l'uis par devers li ferma.
288 Le commun dehors enferma,
Quar il avoit tres grant courage
De consummer son mariage.
Mais il alloit tout aultrement:
292 A s'espouse vint simplement;
Ce ne soi ge s'il se coucha,
Mais unques a lié n'attoucha,
Au meins par dessoubz la ceinture.
296 Ainz fu sa premeraine cure
De Dieu devotement proier [74c]
Qu'il lor voulist grace envoier.
Puis li dist apres sa proiere:
300 »Ma doulce suer, m'amie chiere,

---

266 biens
278 Cellui q.
287 d. lui f.
293 Si ne scei je si se c.

294 l. ne toucha
296 premiere
298 voulsist
299 lui

Il n'est nulle chose qui faille
A qui Dieu creint, ne rien qui vaille
Fors qui Dieu aime, creint et sert.
304 Nul n'a en cest mondain desert
Terme ne trieve de sa vie.
Por ce vos requier, doulce amie,
Tant com au secle demourez,
308 Que Dieu craigniez et honnourez;
Si ne porrez nul aultre creindre.
Et tel crainte vos fera maindre
Es sains cieulx pardurablement,
312 Quant Dieu au jour du Jugement
Rendra a chacun sa desserte.
Si sachiez qu'il n'est nulle perte
De vertu, tant soit eslevee,
316 Qui ne puisse estre recouvree
Fors de soule virginité,
Quar qui la pert, en verité
James virge ne resera,
320 Ne le doulx chant ne chantera
Que les virges tant solement
Chantent devant Dieu noblement
En paradis par excellence;
324 Ne ne sivra par innocence
L'Aignel en touz lieux, droite route.
Moult fait dont grant meschief sans doute
Cil qui pert sa virginité,
328 Quar qui la garde o charité,
Les anges qui o Dieu habitent   [74d]
Comme frere et suer le visitent
En ceste mortel region.
332 Assez tost, se nous voulion,
Perdrion ceste marguerite,
Mais nos aron greignor merite
Et porron trop mielx Dieu ensuivre,
336 Se nos voulon ci virges vivre,
Que se corrumpuz estion.
Quant pour nostre redemption
Le filz Dieu voult de virge nestre
340 Et il eslut por li a estre

---

303 Fort qui Dieu creint laime et sert
340 E. i. esleut p. lui a e.

109

Virge touz temps, c'est grant prouvaille
Qu'il n'est nul estat qui tant vaille.
Ensivon donc, je vos en proie,
344   Par commun accort ceste voie
Et servons a Dieu humblement;
Si pourron chanter lïement
Le doulx chant que les anges chantent
348   Qui devant la majesté hantent.«
       Celle qui estoit cremetouse
Selon nature et vergondouse,
Comme sunt jeunes pucelletes
352   Qui sunt debonnaires et netes
Et legieres a doctriner,
S'accorda a enteriner
Tantost quanqu'il li sermonna.
356   Et cil son anel li donna
Ou il avoit un escarboucle,
Et de sa seinture la boucle
Lïee en un vermeil suaire;
360   Et li dist: »Tant que je repaire,   [75a]
De Dieu servir ne vos tardez,
Et ces joiaulx ci tant gardez
Comme a nostre Seigneur plaira
364   Qui avecques nos parfera.
S'il li plaist, sa misericorde,
Cil mette entre nos tel [a]corde
Qu'il meinge touz temps entre nous;
368   Si ne nos sera point penous
Son service, mes grant delit.«
Apres ces motz lessa le lit,
Et prist tant qu'assez li sembla
372   De la monnoie; et puis s'embla
De ses parens celeement
Et vint a la mer droitement
Ou il trouva tantost passage.
376   Si vint par mi la mer a nage
Au port de Laodice en Sire,
Non pas celle a l'istore dire

---

344 accord
345 servon
355 T. quanqui lui s.   360 lui
356 lui   365 lui
                             371 lui

Ou ja sist l'eglise septime
380 A qui Jhesu Crist fist l'abisme
Escrire de l'Apocalipse.
D'illec s'en alla en Edisse,
Une cité moult allosee
384 Qui estoit Rages appellee
Jadis au temps des Mediëns;
Mais a cel temps de crestiëns
Estoit toute pleine et porprise,
388 Et y avoit moult belle eglise
Ou nom de la Virge Marie.
Illec pensa user sa vie
Saint Alexi en penitance.
392 De quanqu'il avoit fist pitance
Es povres qu'il pot la voier;   [75b]
Puis se commença a soier
En robe chaitive et desprise
396 Avecquez eulx devant l'eglise.
De ce qui por Dieu li venoit
Son corps en vie soustenoit.
S'il avoit point de remenant,
400 Il estoit donné maintenant
Es povres qui o li estoient,
Qui souvent es mains li gardoient.
        Quant le cler jor fut ajorné
404 Apres la nuit que destourné
S'estoit saint Alexi de Romme,
Qui n'emmena coffre ne somme
Ne compaignon en son voiage,
408 Les dames selon lor usage
Vindrent visiter l'espousee;
Mais el estoit si emplouree
Qu'elle ne lor pot nul mot dire.
412 Li plusieurs n'en firent que rire
Qui l'aventure ne savoient,
Et en sobzriant li disoient:
»Dame, ce sunt lermes perdues!
416 Ainsi fumes nos avenues,

381 Escrivre   402 lui
397 lui   412 Lui p.
401 lui   414 lui
379 j. fist l.

Ainsi doivent estre ordenees
Toutes les nouvealx marïees.«
Et el respondit lors a paine:
420   »Se je sui de grant dolour plaine,
Dames, ne m'en vuillez reprendre.
Certes, j'ay uncor a apprendre
Ce dont vos m'avez accusee,
424   Mais de ce suy trop adoulee
Que celli qu'espousé avoie,
Que plus que rien du monde amoie,
Ne soi quel cause il a eü

[75c]

428   Mais ennuit est deci meü
Et m'a, ne soi por quoi, laissee.
James a jour ne seray liee
Si que tant que je le revoye.«
432   Lors fu tantost toute la joie
Des neuces en plour convertie.
Toute Romme fut estourmie;
Chacun le quert, mes nul nel treuve.
436   A honte, ce dient: »Se preuve
Cil qui la flour estoit des sages:
C'est bien voir que de touz aages
Convient redoter par nature.«
440   Le pere, qui fut en grant cure,
Envoia tantost ses messages
Par touz païs, par touz langages,
Por son filz querre et amener;
444   Mais nul ne seult tant pener
Qu'il sceüst de li verité.
Si en ot il en la cité
D'Edisse, et por Dieu li donnerent,
448   Mais unquez point ne l'aviserent;
Et poverté le desguisa.
Et il, qui bien les avisa
Des ce qu'il les vit en l'encloistre,
452   Ne se fist point a eulx cognoistre
Mais dist sans plus a voiz serie:

---

422 encor
425 cellui
431 S. quatant que j.
436 Ce p.
444 sot

445 lui
447 !ui
449 povrete
450 E. lui q.

»Doulx Jhesu Crist, je te mercie,
Qui m'as hui fait aumosne avoir

456   De mes serfs et de mon avoir.«
      Maintes gens qui ne scevent mie   [75d]
Par quelx poins la chevalerie
Des cieulx doit estre demenee,

460   Maintiennent que ceste celee
Qu'il fist de soi es gens son pere
Fu malvestié grande et amere,
Quar s'en li point d'amour eüst

464   Ne de pitié, com il deüst,
Ja ne lessast pere ne mere
Sans allegeance en tel misere
Com il pensoit bien qu'il estoient.

468   Mais celx qui ce dient forvoient,
Quar s'a eulx se fust fait cognoistre
Ilz li eüssent fait descroistre
Ou perir sa devocion,

472   Quar de charnel affection
L'eüssent tempté asprement,
Par qui maint bon commencement
Fault a bonne conclusion:

476   C'est ce qui de religion
Fait souvent maint fol ressortir;
C'est vent ardant qui amortir
Fait la verdour de charité.

480   Si est moult grant necessité
Que de li se sache deffendre
Cil qui veult a Dieu s'ame rendre;
Mais sur touz eschiver le doivent

484   Celx qui cures d'ames reçoivent
Et ensement religieux,
Quar cest vice est malicieux,
Et soubz l'ombre de charité

488   Trait les gens a iniquité.
Comment? il lor fait le bien mendre,   [76a]
Por le greignor delaisser, prendre,
Et puis les y fait tant lïer

492   Qu'il lor en fait Dieu oublïer;

---

461 g. de s. p.   470 lui
463 lui   481 lui
468 dist   492 omblier

Et n'ont entente ne courage
Fors seulement en lor lignage.
Bien est voir trop a cuer amer
496 Qui ses parens ne veult amer,
Mais Dieu le pere souverain
Doit estre amé le premerain
Et servi souverainement.
500 Donc il meïsmes, qui ne ment,
Ces motz en l'Ewangile assigne:
Que celli n'est pas de li digne
Qui aime plus ou pere ou mere,
504 Femme ou enfans ou seur ou frere.
Donc ne se doit de Dieu retraire
Nul por gré a ses parens faire.
      Saint Jeroeme tesmoigne encore
508 En l'epistre a Heliodore
Que nul ne doit pour plour de mere
Ne por gramoïement de pere,
Qui moult est poignant et grevoux,
512 Ne por la pitié des nepvoux,
Ne por charnel appartenance,
Laisser la croiz de penitance;
Quar se noz parens sunt loiaux,
516 Si sunt lors conseilz desloiaux
Volentiers en ceste partie,
Tout soit ce qu'ilz nel voient mie;
De telx y a par aventure.
520 Por ce, quicunques prent la cure
De soi saulver ne doit recroire   [76b]
Por rien qu'ilz facent accroire,
Mais tousjours vertueusement
524 Suivre son bon commencement
Tant que Dieu es cieulx le coronne.
Saint Alexi, dont je sermonne,
Fist donquez a droit et com sage
528 De garder soi de son lignage;
Et s'aucun ne me daigne croire,
Si en croye le Roi de gloire
Qui es sains cieulx, ou il habite,
532 Li en rendit haulte merite

---

502 Q. cellui . . . lui d.   529 men d.
518 ne v.   532 Lui

114

Au partir de cest val de lermes.
Les messagers en plusieurs termes
Et en plusieurs regnes le quistrent.
536 Unquez nouvelles n'en appristrent,
Tant que par ennuy retornerent;
Si distrent bien et affermerent
Qu'en nul païs n'en nulle place
540 Nul ne povoit savoir estrace
Ne de sa mort ne de sa vie.
La mere, qui tant fu marrie
Qu'a poi que de deul ne parti,
544 Des ce que son filz s'en parti
De son païs si faictement,
Mist un sac sur le pavement
De sa chambre por faire lit.
548 Unque puis a greignor delit
Ne voult jesir ne nuit ne jour.
La se dolosoit sans sejour
Et disoit: »James en ma vie
552 Ne demeinray envoiserie,
Ne de cest lit ci ne mouvray   [76c]
Si je n'ay ançois recouvray
Mon doulx enfant que tant amoie
556 Qui estoit ma vie et ma joie,
Mon confort, mon soustenement.«
Et la bru disoit ensement:
»Tant que j'aye eu de li nouvelle,
560 Aussi come la turterelle
A qui son pareil ne repaire
Seray et triste et solitaire.«
        Ainsi por li dolens estoient
564 Touz ceulx qui charnelment l'amoient.
Et il por tout le monde oroit
A Edisse ou il demoroit
En un portal devant l'eglise.
568 Moult avoit lit d'estrange guise
Qu'il ne l'avoit jadis a Romme,
Quar il prenoit un moult cort somme
Long temps apres l'anuitement,
572 Tout vestu, sur le pavement;

559 lui   564 charnelement
563 lui   565 tant

115

N'y avoit coite ne courtines.
Et si levoit devant matines
Qu'il odit en toutes saisons;
576 Puis reprenoit ses oraisons,
A nuz genoulz devotement
Estendu sur le pavement,
Tant que gens au moustier venissent;
580 Quar ja en cel point nel veïssent
En assemblees ne en presses.
Au dimenche, apres les messes,
Recevoit le saint sacrement
584 Du corps Dieu moult devotement
Tousjours puis par l'acoustumance. [76d]
Quant il ot ceste penitance
Dis [et] set ans touz pleins fournie,
588 L'ymage a la Virge Marie
Dist a cil qui gardoit l'eglise:
»Met ens l'omme Dieu que Dieu prise,
Quar il est digne et convenable
592 D'avoir le regne pardurable;
Saint Esperit en li habite.
Son oraison est si eslite
Qu'el est tantost a Dieu montee.«
596 Lors fu celli en grant pencee
Por qui l'image ce disoit,
Quar de nul ne s'en advisoit.
Et l'image reprist a dire:
600 »Il est la hors ou cimetire.«
Atant a cil sans demoree
La porte souef deffermee:
Saint Alexi trouva orant:
604 Si le mist ens tout en plorant
Et li porta grant reverence.
L'endemain ne fist pas silence
Du miracle qu'il ot veü;
608 Par ce fu tantost cogneü
Saint Alexi en la cité.
Nul ne le tint puis en vi[l]té,
Chacun le prist a honourer;
612 Mais il n'y voult plus demourer,

590 Mete e. lomme q. D. p.   600 cimetere
593 S. Esperit e. lui h.   605 lui
596 celui   606 L. si n.

116

Quar l'en li porta reverence
Et il cremut sa conscïence
Qu'el n'en fust aucun poi blecee
616 Ou sa merite amen[u]isee.

Ceulx qui en la glore celeste [77a]
Attendent lor los et lor feste
N'ont cure d'estre ci loez,
620 Et nous, qui sommes emboëz
De pechiez, voulon sans raison
Avoir y los: c'est l'achaison
De bailler libelle d'injure;
624 Quar, certes, qui ne fust en cure
D'avoir ici vaine loënge,
Il n'y sentist nulle laidenge
Plus que saint Alexi sentoit
628 Qui de cel païs s'absentoit
Affin qu'il n'y fust honouré.
Povre, maigre et descoulouré
S'en retorna a Laodice,
632 Et cuida aller en Cilice,
D'illeques, a saint Pol de Tharse.
Mais le vent fist en mer la farse
Es mariniers qui le porterent,
636 Quar au port rommain arriverent.
Quant il vit ce, Dieu mercia,
A tout par li dist: »Plus n'y a;
En l'ostel mon pere seray,
640 James aultre ne changeray.«

Lors vint a la cité de Romme;
Unquez n'y fu cogneü d'omme
Ne festoié ne salué,
644 Quar il ert povre et esnué;
Ne treuve gaires qui l'accole.
Au retorner du Capitole
Encontra o grant compaignie
648 Son pere qui nel cognut mie,
Mais il lui bien cogneü a. [77b]
A genoillons le salua,
Et ne l'osa pere appeler:
652 »Or sergant Dieu, fay hosteler,«

---

613 lui p.   626 sentit nulle nulle l.
618 Attende   638 lui

Dist il, »cest pelerin estrange
En ton hostel, et nel me change;
Mais de ton relief me fai vivre.
656   Que Dieu, qui a cent doubles livre
Les merites de bien donné,
Por quoi qu'il soit abandonné
De loial cuer et d'enterin,
660   Ait pitié de ton pelerin
Et t'en envoit joie fournie.«
Le pere qui ne cognut mie
Son filz qui l'ostel demanda,
664   Por l'amor du filz commanda,
Comme Dieu l'avoit ordené,
Qu'il fust a son hostel mené;
Et lieu propre li assigna
668   Ou il beut et ou il disna;
Et a un vallet ensement
Commanda il estroitement
Qu'il li porveïst de sa vie
672   Et qu'il ne l'entroubliast mie.
     Si com un povre pelerin
Devers Grece ou d'oultre le Rin
Remaint cil en l'ostel son pere.
676   Unquez d'espouse ne de mere
Ne d'aultre n'y fu cogneü.
Mal couchié fut et mal peü,
Tout nel voulist le seignor mie,
680   Quar de li avoient envie
Tous les serjans de la maison.   [77c]
Souvente faiz sans achaison
De l'eau[e] chaulde le cuisoient
684   Et sur la teste li getoient
Les ordures de la cuisine;
Ou en lieu d'autre discipline,
Par les garez d'une escuëlle
688   Ou d'un pestel ou d'une astelle
Avoit, quant il passoit devant.
Ja n'en allast noise mouvant

---

661 envoie j.   673 comme
667 lui a.   679 voulsist
671 lui   680 lui
672 entroublast m.   684 lui g.

Ne ja pleinte n'en fust oÿe.
692 Ses oroisons a voiz serie,
Ses abstinences et ses veilles,
Ou il estoit fort a merveilles,
Continuoit en pacïence.
696 Il portoit a touz reverence
Et n'estoit de nul honnouré.
Quant il ot ainsi demouré
Dis [et] set ans en penitance
700 Chiez son pere sans cognoissance,
Le feu roi des Goz, Raagaiz,
Qui en son temps fist moult d'agaiz
Et maint grief a crestïenté,
704 Vint en Ytale a grant plenté
De gens crueulx et duiz de guerre,
Quar bien cuidoit Romme conquerre
O le grant effors de sa route.
708 Les Rommains, qui furent en doubte
De li et de sa cruaulté,
Firent lors en generaulté
A touz les crestïens proier
712 Que Dieu lor voulist envoier
Secours par sa misericorde   [77d]
Contre celle gent ville et orde
Qui a tort les envaïssoient.
716 Un jour de di[e]menche oroient
A Saint Pere pour cest affaire,
Si oïrent ou sainctuaire
Apres la messe droitement
720 Une voiz disant clerement:
»Venez a moi qui labourez
Et qui ou travail demourez,
Et je vos referay sans doubte.«
724 Tantost la compaignie toute
Kirïe eleïson distrent
Et en prostration se mistrent.
    Tant diz com en prostracion
728 Estoient par devocion,

---

691 oirye   716 jours
709 lui   722 en t.
712 voulsist
705 creucelx

La voiz parla segondement:
»Querez l'omme Dieu prestement
Qui por la cité de Romme oure,
732 Quar il trespassera en l'oure
Et de cest secle a Dieu ira,
Quant le saint jour esclargira
De la Saincte Croiz aouree.«
736 Quant venue fut l'ajournee,
Grans et petiz a Dieu oroient
A l'eglise, ou venuz estoient
Li plusieurs nuz piez et en haire,
740 Que Jhesu Crist lor daignast faire
De cel saint homme demonstrance.
Et la voiz lor dist en oïance:
»En la maison Eufemïen
744 Querez icel bon crestïen.«
    Tantost apres ceste parole   [78a]
Innocent, qui fut apostole,
N'a illeques plus demouré;
748 Avec Archade et Honnouré,
Qui adonc l'empire garderent,
Chiez Eufemïen s'en allerent
Por celi dont besoing avoient.
752 Uns et autres li demandoient
Qui estoit cil de sa maison
Dont Dieu prisoit tant l'oraison,
Et il disoit qu'il ne savoit.
756 Adonc le valet qui avoit
Saint Alexi a pourvoier
Li dist: »Sire, faictes voier
Que ce ne soit cel pelerin,
760 Quar je ne scey plus acerin
Ne plus parfait en pacïence,
Et est homme de grant science;
Et merveilles de saincte vie:
764 Je ne vien de nulle partie
Que tousjors ne le truisse ourant.«
Lors alla le pere courant
La ou il avoit son repeire;

---

739 Lui   752 lui
741 cest   758 Lui
751 celui

120

768	Si trouva son filz mort en beire
	Encore tout entiedissant,
	Le voult cler et resplendissant,
	Qu'il tint a merveilleuse chose,
772	Et une chartre en la main close
	Ou tout le proces de sa vie,
	Si comme vos l'avez oïe,
	Avoit ainz son trespassement
776	Escript de sa main proprement
	Par divine ammonicion.
	Le pere sans dillacion
	Por la chartre avoir se bessa,
780	Mais cil mie ne [la] li lessa,
	Ainz la tint assez fermement.
	Lors retourna isnellement
	Le pere compter ceste chose
784	Au pape et es filz Theodose.
	Touz ensemble lors retornerent
	Au corps saint et moult regarderent
	Celle chartre en sa main roulee,
788	Sa clere face enluminee
	Qui come estelle reluisoit.
	Et Eufemïen disoit:
	»Vez ci un pelerin estrange
792	Qui a tout nuz piez et en lange
	Ceens dis [et] set ans geü,
	Et si n'a point esté sceü
	Dont il est né, ne de quel terre,
796	Quar il ne nos chaloit d'enquerre
	De li por sa simple personne;
	Au jor d'uy encor entor nonne
	Ne savion qu'il fust malade.«
800	Lors dist l'emperëour Archade:
	»Tout soion nos vilz pechëors
	Si sommes nos emperëours
	De par Dieu, et moi et mon frere;
804	Et cil pape, c'est chose clere,
	A de par Dieu la cure emprise
	Et la garde de saincte eglise.

[78b]

---

769 E. t. entreluisant   800 emperour
795 e. ne d.   802 emperours
797 lui

Si vait avant, plus n'y delaye,
808   Celle chartre du poing li traye;
Si saron que nos devon faire.«   [78c]
Atant li alla du poing traire
L'apostole moult humblement,
812   Et le trespassé bonnement
Li laissa sans contretenir.
Lors firent touz en paiz tenir
Tant que l'en eüst leu la chartre.
816   Quant le pere oït en quel chartre
Avoit esté en sa maison
Son enfant si longue saison,
Par grant angoisse se pasma.
820   Au revenir moult se blasma
Que entretant n'avoit pris garde:
»Hé! las«, dist il, »quant je regarde,
Beau filz, que tu es trespassé,
824   Bien est tout mon espoir passé
Du bien que de toi attendoie.
James ou monde n'avray joie
Quant devant moi te voi gesant
828   En la biere mu et tesant.
Las, por quoi ne me revelas,
Quant ceenz o nos t'ostelas,
Que tu nostre cher filz estoies?
832   Certes, pas souffrir ne devoies,
Ce soi ge bien, par ta desserte,
La paine que tu as soufferte.«
       La mere de l'autre partie
836   Crioit comme femme marrie,
Sur le corps de son filz plourant:
»Hei! Mort, que vas tu demourant
Que tu ne prens ceste chestive!
840   Quar james, tant comme je vive,
Je n'avray liesce ne joye,   [78d]
Quar j'ay perdu quanque j'avoye
Ne ja ne sera recouvré.
844   Hei! filz, pour quoi as tu ouvré
Envers nos ainsi cruëlment?

---

808 lui   838 He
810 lui   844 He
813 Lui   845 cruellement

Tu nos vëoies en dement
Et souvent por toi lermoïer,
848   Si ne daignoies desploïer
Ne demonstrer qui tu estoies,
Mes de tes serjans enduroies
Touz despiz et toutes injures.
852   Trop seront mes mes paines dures
Et mes angoisses trop ameres.
Plourez o moi, chaistives meres,
Quar j'ay dis [et] set ans eü
856   Comme povre mescogneü
Mon cher enfant en ma maison,
Et unques par nulle achaison
Ne le cogneu, lasse, dolente.«
860   L'espouse qui estoit presente
Et n'estoit, puis la departie
De li , de sa mere partie,
Menoit telx plours et telx crïees
864   Qu'el faisoit de lermes plourees
A maint homme mouiller la chape.
Les emperëours et le pappe
Le corps en une biere mistrent
868   Et o un cardinal le pristrent
Por porter a Saint Boniface;
Mais tant avoit gens en la place
Que forment les empeschoient,
872   Quar de toutes pars acouroient
ᵐar devocion au proudomme   [79a]
Qui devoit prier Dieu por Romme.
Ne lor chaloit d'estre batuz
876   Ou entre les piez abatuz,
Ne de recuillir la monnoie
Que l'en getoit par mi la voie,
Mais qu'il touchassent a la biere.
880   Les enfers de quelque maniere
En un moment gariz estoient,
Si tost com toucher y povoient.
Et apres par set jours entiers
884   Qu'il jut sur terre, en dementiers

---

852 T. s. mes p. d.
862 De lui do s. m. p.

861 p. de la d.   862 D. l. do s.

Que l'en faisoit sa sepoulture,
Il nessoit une odour si pure
Du corps de li et si tres saine
888 Que ce sembloit une arche plaine
Du meillor aromat du monde
Ou basme qui en Inde habonde.
Le roi Radaigaiz entretant
892 Alloit Ytaille soubzmettant
A son povair si qu'en Tusquenne,
Et celx qui la foi crestienne
Maintenoient faisoit occire.
896 Archade, qui le grief martire
De ses gens ne pot endurer,
S'alla donques aventurer,
Et prist a certaine journee
900 Avec li bataille arrestee;
Mais il avoit moult grant fiance
Que Dieu prendroit du roi vengeance
Par les oraisons de l'eglise.
904 Quant vint a la bataille assise,
Les crestïens Dieu reclamerent,   [79b]
Quar lors ennemiz moult doubterent
Por ce que trop grant nombre furent.
908 Et Gotz par grant orguil s'esmurent
En grant espoir de desconfire
Touz les crestïens de l'empire.
Mais par le divin adjutore
912 Les Rommains ourent la victore
Si tresnoble et si glorieuse
Qu'onquez n'y ot plaie greveuse
Nul des Rommains qui combatirent,
916 Et plus de cent mille mourirent
Des Goz ou champ de la bataille;
Ne unquez le prix d'une maille
Ne valut au roi sa posnee,
920 Quar en meïsmes la journee
Fut il pris et puis mort a honte.
Ceste victore que je compte
Tesmoigne bien en verité

---

887 lui
893 Tusquane
900 lui

924	Ou quint livre de la Cité
	Saint Augustin, qui fait a croire.
	Nonporquant, c'est bien chose voire,
	Il ne dit pas par quel merite,
928	Mais el doit estre a cest escript,
	Ce me semble, especiaulment,
	Quant Dieu voult que principaulment
	L'oraison de li fust requise
932	Por le peril de saincte eglise;
	Et puis par sa misericorde
	De la guerre que je recorde
	Lor envoia si grant lïesce;
936	Quar unquez par mortel prouesce
	Ce n'avint sans divin suffrage
	Qu'en bataille eüst tel dommage
	Et tel meschief l'une partie
940	Que cent mille y perdissent vie,
	Et en l'autre sains demourassent
	Si que nul mehaing n'en portassent.
	Cassïen dit apertement
944	Que poi vault bon commencement
	Qui semblable fin n'y adjouste.
	C'est chose qui gaires ne couste,
	Si com saint Gregore devise,
948	Que celli richesces despise
	Qui a son voloir en exploite;
	Mais c'est forte chose et dest[r]oite,
	Quant homme a lessé sa richesce
952	Et il est povre et en destresce
	Et despit en bourg et en ville,
	Qu'il tienge lors la chose a ville
	Dont il avoit fait cession.
956	Se Dieu en la temptacion
	Par sa grace ne li desclaire,
	De legier tantost y repaire
	En apert ou segretement;
960	Si pert son bien oultreement
	Qu'il avoit commencé a faire;
	Quar l'Ewangile nos desclaire

[79c]

---

931 d. lui
945 semblent
948 Qui 954 c. abille

957 lui
960 bon

Que cil sauf solement sera
964   Qui en bien persevera.
Si ne devon por nulle cause
Ou service Dieu faire pause,
Quar si comme Cassïen pose,
968   Cil retourne qui se repose;
Dont un exemple vos diron: [79d]
Celli qui nage a l'aviron
Contre le cours de la riviere,
972   S'il se cesse en nulle maniere
Qu'il ne nage tousjors a ourne,
Le cours de l'eau le retourne
Tantost plus qu'il n'avoit nagié.
976   Aussi est tout descouragié
Du bien qu'il commence par faire
Celli qui au monde repaire,
Depuis qu'il li a clos sa porte;
980   Quar le cours du monde l'emporte
Plus en un seul jour la moitié
Qu'en un an n'avoit esploitié.
Si peut prendre bon exemplaire
984   Qui veult perseverance faire,
Au proces de saint Alexi,
Qui si bien la soue texi
Qu'a touz deliz qu'il povoit prendre
988   Il ne voult unquez la main tendre
Puis la delessance premiere.
Dieu nos vuille par sa priere
Nos pechiez icy pardonner
992   Et puis avec li couronner.
AMEN

969 Donc
970 Celui
978 Celui
979 lui
989 le

126

NOTES

1-6. In chapter XIV of the Acts of the Apostles, Saint Paul and Barnabas pass through divers provinces (Derbe, Lystra, Iconium, and Antioch) visiting the faithful and confirming the churches. Verses 1-6 of our text seem directly inspired by chapter XIV, 21. Cf.: »Fortifiant le courage des disciples, les exhortant à persévérer dans la foi, et leur représentant que c'est par beaucoup de peines et d'afflictions que nous devons entrer dans le royaume de Dieu.«

7. Prosper of Aquitaine (Saint), historian, poet and Latin theologian (circa 390-circa 460), crusader against Pelagianism, doctrine which denied original sin and maintained the freedom of the will and its power to attain righteousness. His works are contained in J.-P. Migne, *Patrologiae*, Tomus LI, entitled *Sancti Prosperi Aquitani, Opera Omnia*. Cf. also L. Valentin, *Saint Prosper d'Aquitaine* (Paris & Toulouse, 1900).

44-61. Cf. le Livre de la Sagesse, chapitre V, 3-14: »Ils diront en eux-mêmes, étant touchés de regret, et jetant des soupirs dans le serrement de leurs coeurs: Ce sont ceux-là qui ont été autrefois l'objet de nos railleries, et que nous donnions pour exemple de personnes dignes de toutes sortes d'opprobres. (3)
Insensés que nous étions, leur vie nous paroissoit une folie, et leur mort honteuse! (4)
Cependant les voilà élevés au rang des enfants de Dieu, et leur partage est avec les saints. (5)
De quoi nous a servi notre orgueil? qu'avons-nous tiré de la vaine ostentation de nos richesses? (8)
Toutes ces choses sont passées comme l'ombre, et comme un courrier qui court, (9)
Ou comme un oiseau qui vole (see v. 57 of our poem) au travers de l'air, sans qu'on puisse remarquer par où il passe . . . (11)
Ainsi nous ne sommes pas plus tôt nés que nous avons cessé d'être; nous n'avons pu montrer en nous aucune trace de vertu et nous avons été consumés par notre malice. (13)
Voilà ce que les pécheurs diront dans l'enfer: (14) . . . Cf. v. 61.

52. Towards the end of the 13th century, tonic *eulx* started to replace, little by little, the accented nominative plural *il* just as tonic *lui* began to replace the accented nominative singular *il*. See Schwan-Behrens, # 322,3. Cf. note for v. 649.

67. Cf. the note for verses 44-61.

94-97. *Le Livre de Chevalerie*. Reference to Jean de Meun's translation (1284)[1] of Vegetius' (latin writer, end of 4th century, A.D.) *Re Militari* (Traité de l'art militaire). See *L'Art de Chevalerie*, Ulysse Robert, ed. (Paris, Société des anciens textes français, 1897). Our poet is probably referring to Book III, chapter XXVI, entitled »Ci parole

---

1 See *L'Art de Chevalerie*, Introduction, p. viii.

127

le XXVIe chapitres qui enseigne rieulles generaus de batillier;« and more specifically to the following passage on page 131: »Ne maine jamais chevalier en commune bataille, se tu ne vois avant qu'il ait esperance de victoire.« Cf. the note for verses 136-143.

104. *Aglaes* must be disyllabic or else the verse has nine syllables. Cf. the 13th century version where *Aglaël* 124, 578, is trisyllabic: Aglaël, sa molhier, l'a pris a reconteir: (124)/ Ne sa mere [A]glaël ke fust sa porteüre (578). See my edition entitled "The Oxford Version of the *Vie de saint Alexis*: An Old French Poem of the Thirteenth Century", *Romania*, Tome 92, 1971, pages 1-36. Cf. MS. 2162 (P) of the 13th century version where Aglaël is again trisyllabic: Aglaël, sa mollier, le prent a raconter: (133)/ Ne sa mere Aglaël qui en fist sa porture (690). Aglaes is also trisyllabic (Ki Aglaes aveit a non) in the 11th century poem published by Gaston Paris, »La Vie de St. Alexis«, *Romania*, VIII (1879), 163-180.

132. As E. Walberg pointed out (p. 151), this term is frequently employed to symbolize hypocrisy, falsity. Cf. the allegorical poem *Le Roman de Fauvel* by Gervais du Bus[2] (beginning of the 14th century). See the Introduction, p. iv, where the author defines what the horse Fauvel signifies: »Il faut d'abord parler de sa couleur, car Aristote a bien raison de déclarer que les accidents aident fort à connaître la substance (v. 180) . . . Fauvel est composé de *faus* et de *vel* (voile). Les six lettres de son nom sont, en outre, les initiales de Flatterie, Avarice, Vilenie, Variété, Envie, Lâcheté (v. 256).«

136-143. Cf. the note for verses 94-97. These verses seem inspired by Book II, chapter 1, p. 5-6. Cf.: »Car la science de ce qui appartient as batailles nourrist hardement de batillier . . . et grans multitude de gens rudes (see verses 137 and 138 of our poem) qui riens n'ont appris d'armes est tous jours abandonnee a occision et a peril.« (p. 6)

140. Rare example of this substantive derived from the verb *exerciter* (s'exercer à, exercer, exécuter, etc.). See Godefroy, *Lexique de l'ancien français*, p. 221. Cf. *exercité* 67 (=exercé) in *L'Art de Chevalerie*.

167. *ses porsoians*=those who possess her (=scïence, v. 164).

188. E. Walberg (p. 151) refers to this verse to point out our author's lack of concentration and considers such digressions as his main literary weakness as a poet. We must be lenient, however, and remember the great predilection of medieval authors for *digressio*. Few of them have not sinned, at some time or other, with respect to this popular medieval stylistic device. I do not believe, however, as he apparently does, that our poet is seriously reproaching himself in this verse with regard to *digressio*.

231. *doloreux voie*; see Morphology, Substantive and Adjective.

251. For more information on *bruman*, derived from the Old Nordic brúdmann, see E. Walberg in *Studia neophilologia*, XVI (1943-44), p. 39-49.

278. I believe that E. Walberg, in spite of his great knowledge of Old French, is gravely mistaken here (p. 151). *Celli* is the subject of the reflexive verb *s'embla* 280 (preterite 3 of s'embler, slip away), and not the indirect object of *sembla assez* (v. 280). Cf. . . . et puis s'embla (v. 372). See the Glossary and, in particular, the Morphology, Demonstratives.

293. *soi*=sai; cf. verses 427, 429, 833. See Glossary.

---

2 Published by Arthur Langfors, Paris, 1919 (Société des anciens textes français).

303. *qui*=à celui qui.

324. I believe that the MS. reads *sivra* instead of *suira* (selected by Walberg). Likewise *ensivon* 343, not *ensuion*. See Glossary and Morphology, Present Indicative.

356. *son anel*, id est, his wedding ring: See note for v. 358.

357. Although *escarboucle* (derived from *escarboncle*, masc. and fem., by analogy with *boucle*) is usually feminine in Old French, it does appear sporadically as a masculine noun. See Godefroy, Complément; also *Roland*: Et Tervagant tolent son escarboncle 2589; and R. Grandsaignes d'Hauterive, *Dictionnaire d'ancien français*, p. 234: Dunat sun helme e s'escarbuncle.

358. By handing over to his young bride his nuptial ring and *la boucle* (de sa seinture), symbol of his nobility, Alexis is symbolically severing all natural and human bonds which could impede his spiritual growth (his *imitatio Christi*). His saintly program must entail a complete surrender of himself to God, a complete severance with the carnal and ephemeral things of this world to achieve perfect conformity with the Divine Will. The life of a saint is nothing else but the progressive victory of the supernatural over the natural. Everything else must be subordinated to it: love of wife, family, terrestrial goods, glory, etc. See note for verses 500-504 and also note for verses 507 ff. Cf. "The Humanity of Saint Alexis", *Revue belge de Philologie et d'Histoire*, v. XLIX, 1971, p. 865.

378. *a l'istore dire*=according to history. See Walberg, p. 152.

379-381. As Walberg points out (p. 152), the MS. form *fist* is undoubtedly a scribal mistake. Our copyist must have thought that *septime* referred to a person (=Ou ja Septime fist l'eglise) and not to the Church of *Laodiciae*, the seventh of the churches enumerated in the Apocalypse of Saint John the Divine, Chapter I, 11: »Un dimanche, je fus ravi en esprit, et j'entendis derrière moi une voix forte et éclatante comme une trompette, (10) Qui disoit: Ecrivez dans un livre ce que vous voyez, et envoyez-le aux sept Eglises qui sont dans l'Asie, à Ephèse, à Smyrne, à Pergame, à Thyatire, à Sardes, à Philadelphie, et à Laodicée.« (11)

384. *Rages*=ancient name of the city of Edessa. Cf. the 13th century version of the *Vie de saint Alexis* where we find *Rohais* 330, 364, 473. The form *Rohais* appears for the city of Edessa in many medieval texts based on the Latin legend while the earlier 11th century version has *Alsis* 86, 93, 113, 158, 382 (MS. L; see Gaston Paris, *La Vie de saint Alexis* (Paris, 1966), *Arsis* (MS. A), *Axis* (MS. P), *Aussi* (MS. S), and *Alis* (MS. M). All these forms go back to the original *Alsis*, but just how *Edessus* became *Alsis* is difficult to ascertain[3]. However, in the *Vie de saint Alexis* published in *Romania*, VIII, 173, v. 306: . . . Qui ore est Rohès apelee.

402. This verse seems to mean that the poor who were with Alexis often looked into his hands (es mains) to see whether he had something (point de remenant, v. 399) to give to them.

412. The masculine form *li plusieurs*, referring to *Les dames* 408, is rather singular. However, the masculine nominative plural forms *il, ils/ilz*, are sporadically used in place of the feminine form *eles*, a trait characteristic of the West or North. See Pope, # 1251, and Morphology, Personal Pronouns.

418. *les nouvealx mariees* (=OF les nouvelles mariees), brings to mind the MF une fille nouveau-née, une gloire nouveau-née, etc. See Walberg, p. 152.

---

3 See Gaston Paris et L. Pannier. *La vie de St. Alexis* (Paris, 1872), p. 180.

428. Note the common OF omisssion of the reflexive pronoun *se* in compound tenses.

444. I believe that the MS. reads *seult*, not *soult* (selected by Walberg). See Glossary.

446. *en=ses messages* (v. 441).

449. *poverté* (< paupertatem), variant form of OF *poverte* (< *pauperta).

489-490. Syntaxe décousue=Comment? il lor fait prendre le bien mendre por delaisser le greignor.

500-504. Cf. the 13th century version of the *Vie de saint Alexis*: »Qui plus aime ne pere ne mere ne parent,/ Fil ne mollier ne terre, honor ne casement,/ Que moi dist nostre Sires, ne mon commandement,/ Il n'est dignes de moi ne a moi ne s'atent« (MS. 2162, vv. 207-210). Cf. also Le Saint Evangile de Jésus-Christ selon Saint Matthieu, chapitre X, 37: »Celui qui aime son père ou sa mère plus que moi, n'est pas digne de moi; et celui qui aime son fils ou sa fille plus que moi, n'est pas digne de moi.«

507 ff., verses inspired by Saint Jerome's famous *Epistola ad Heliodorum*. This letter (XIV) was written in the first bitterness of separation and reproaches Heliodorus for having gone back from the perfect way of the ascetic life. Cf. particularly paragraphs 2 and 3 of Letter XIV: "... He that is not with me is against me, and he that gathereth not with me scattereth." (Matt. XII, 30) ... Remember the day on which you enlisted, when, buried with Christ in baptism, you swore fealty to Him, declaring that for His sake you would spare neither father nor mother ... Should your little nephew (Ne por la pitié des nepvoux, v. 512 of our text) hang on your neck, pay no regard to him; should your mother with ashes on her hair and garments rent show you the breasts at which she nursed you, heed her not; should your father prostrate himself on the threshold, trample him under foot and go your way (see verses 510-511). With dry eyes fly to the standard of the cross. In such cases cruelty is the only true affection." (# 2)
"... Scripture, you will argue, bids us obey our parents (Ephesians, VI, 1). Yes, but whoso loves them more than Christ loses his own soul (Matt., X, 37). The enemy takes sword in hand to slay me, and shall I think of a mother's tears (see v. 509 of our poem)? ... The battering ram of natural affection must recoil powerless from the wall of the Gospel. "My mother and my brethren are these whosoever do the will of my Father which is in heaven" (Luke, VIII, 21; Matt., XII, 50). If they believe in Christ let them bid me God-speed, for I go to fight in His name. And if they do not believe, let the dead bury their dead." (Matt., VIII, 22). (# 3) (Translation by the Hon. W. H. Fremantle[4])

519. *Telx* refers to *lors conseilz desloiaux* 516.

532. *li* refers to Saint Alexis.

543. =She very nearly died of grief.

554. *recouvray*=recouvré; see Phonology, Vowels (A).

559. *eu* must be monosyllabic or else the verse has 9 syllables. See *leu* 815, below.

560. The legend of la *tourterelle* is well known in medieval literature. It is said that once she has lost her mate, she never accepts another, nor does she ever place herself on

---

4 See *A Select Library of Nicene and Post-Nicene Fathers of the Christian Church*, v. VI, p. 14-15. Cf. also Migne, *Patrologiae*, Tomus XXII, pages 347-355, for Sancti Hieronymi Epistola XIV ad Heliodorum Monachum.

a green branch or on green shrubbery, symbol of life's renaissance in the springtime, of hope, fertility, and the richness and blossoming of love.

Cf. the thirteenth century version, Laisse LIV, verses 1077-1084:

> »Amis,« ce dist s'espeuse, »or sui venue a jor
> Que trestote ma joie est mue en tristor.
> A loi de toterele qui eskive verdor,
> Deduirai mais mon cors et vivrai en labor,
> N'escouterai mais cant ne ne porterai flor,
> Ne desir mais del siecle le joie ne l'onor.
> A tos jors arai mais vest[e]üre de plor,
> Tors jors serai mais veve, n'ai soing d'atre signor.«

Cf. also the 11th century version: Des or vivrai en guise de tortrele:/ Quant n'ai ton fil, ensemble o tei vueil estre.« (vv. 149-150 of Gaston Paris' edition of the *Vie de saint Alexis*, p. 6.)

568. *estrange*=very different; see Glossary.

580. *Quar*=que: in order that, so that.

589. *a cil qui*; this is the only example of *cil* (nom.) replacing *cel* (oblique); however, note *por celi* 751. See Morphology, Demonstratives.

596. *celli* refers to *cil qui gardoit l'eglise* 589, id est, the sexton.

598. =For with respect to this (*en*), he was thinking of no one, id est, he had no one in mind.

610. For *vi[l]té*, see Phonology, Consonants (L).

633. Saint Alexis was attracted to Tarsus (birthplace of Saint Paul, the apostle) by its famous sanctuary consecrated to Saint Paul.

Verses 628-636 should be compared with the Vita S. Alexii Confessoris (the Latin prose legend) which I have included in the Appendix, q.v., to facilitate comparison with our text. Cf.: 5 . . . & isdem homo Dei ab hominibus venerari coepisset, humanam fugiens gloriam, occulte exiit de civitate Edessa, & venit Laodiciam, ibique navem ascendens volebat in Tharsum Ciliciae ire, ut in templo S. Pauli, quod ibidem est, maneret incognitus. Deo itaque dispensante rapta est navis vento, & ducta est ad Romanum portum. (69-73)

646-648. Cf. *Vita*: » . . . & exiens venit, & obviavit patri suo redeunti a palatio, circumdato obsequentium multitudine . . .« (76-77).

From the standpoint of the researcher, there are many reasons to believe that the home of the legend was not Rome but rather New-Rome, id est, Constantinople. Alexis sets sail in the immediate vicinity of his father's house, and the violent storm which occurs as he is returning directs the course of the boat to his father's home. Neither of these two events would be possible with an inland city. A storm is scarcely imaginable in which a ship on the way from Laodicae in Syria to Tharsus in Cilicia would be driven into the Tyrrhenian Sea. However, it would be much more possible in the Hellespont. Of course, not everything in a legend need be actually possible or factual. The geographical descriptions, however, in the legend are all rather exact; only those which refer to Italian Rome are somewhat obscure. Furthermore, it has been ignored up to now that the name Constantinople occurs in the older texts. The Codex Vallicensis, collated by the Bollandists, says: "descendit autem Capolim, ascendensque navem;" to which the editors have added: "forte voluit Neapolim dicere." It just so happens that the word Cpolis or Kpolis is the customary abbreviation for Constantinople and even the Bollandists use this abbreviation. Of course, even some old copiers have misunderstood the term and have written Nicopolis instead (taking Ni for K) or have written Capitolium (see v. 646 of our poem), thinking of the hill of Rome, whose location is not suited for boarding ships. Another point in favor of the Greek homeland is that the names of the main characters are Greek. Not only that, but Greek words were preserved even in the Latin texts. Thalamus and paramonarius appear in almost all the texts; in some even elemosina, senodochion, ycon, basilica. See my article entitled »Les Origines de la Légende de saint Alexis« which will appear soon in the fall »fascicule« of *Revue belge de Philologie et d'Histoire,*1973. Cf. also M. Rösler, *Sankt Alexius*, (Halle/Saale, 1941), pp. viii-x.

649. *lui*, accusative of the tonic personal pronoun, used instead of the atonic form *le*. See note for v. 52, and Schwan-Behrens, # 322,1, and # 323.

654. *nel me change*=do not make me move, id est, go live elsewhere. Cf.: En l'ostel mon pere seray,/ James aultre ne changeray.« (vv. 639-640)

656-57. =So that God, who compensates in a hundredfold measure the good that we have done . . .

700. *sans cognoissance*=without being recognized.

701. For the etymological form *feu* (=fel), see Morphology, Substantive and Adjective. Concerning *Raagaiz* (Radaigaiz 891), see note for vv. 923-925.

714-715. *celle gent ville et orde* . . . =the Ostrogoths.

721-723. Verses inspired by the Gospel of Saint Matthew, XI, 28: »Venez à moi, vous tous qui êtes fatigués et qui êtes chargés, et je vous soulagerai.« Cf. *Vita*: »Venite ad me omnes, qui laboratis, & onerati estis, & ego vos reficiam.« (100-101)

724-726. Cf. *Vita*: »Qua voce audita, nimio timore territi ceciderunt omnes in facies suas, clamantes; Kyrie eleison.« (101-102)

730-735. Cf. *Vita*: »Quaerite hominem Dei, ut oret pro Roma; illucescente enim die parasceve Deo spiritum reddidit.« (103-104) Cf. the 13th century version where the heavenly voice speaking for the second time merely announces the imminent death of Saint Alexis, but not on Friday: »Car cel josdi promier par sonc l'abe del jor/ Rendra s'arme la belle es mains nostre creator.« (vv. 744-745)
As Walberg points out (p. 154), it is not clear, in our text, whether the poet is referring to the Finding of the Holy Cross (May 3) or to the Exaltation of the Holy Cross (September 14). In the *Vita*, the author is even less specific (illucescente die parasceve) and we may even postulate that the accomplishment of Alexis' death took place on Good Friday if we so desire, thus resulting in an even more perfect »imitatio Christi«. See "The Humanity of Saint Alexis . . .", p. 865.

771. *Qu'il tint*=Ce qu'il tint.

798. *nonne*, the fifth of the seven canonical hours, or the service for it, originally fixed for the ninth hour of the day (or 3 P.M.).

815. Unlike Walberg, I prefer to place the dieresis on eüst rather than on *leu*. In any case, the choice must be made or else the verse has + 1 syllable.
Note that in our poem, the reader of the *chartre* is not specifically mentioned (Tant que l'en eüst leu la chartre). In the 11th century version, he is simply referred to as *li chanceliers* (v. 376). Cf.: »Li chanceliers, cui li mestiers en eret,/ Cil list la chartre; li altre l'escolterent. (vv. 376-377). However, in the 13th century version, *Essïo* (vv. 900, 904), the *maistre cancelier* (899) is expressly designated as the reader of

the *chartre* in verses 901 and 904. Cf.: Essïo ot a non, s'ot le cuer large et sain,/ Cil le list en oiant tot le peule romain. (vv. 900-901); and Laisse XLV: Essïo list la cartre qui bien en fu apris, (904).

859. *cogneu*=cognui; see Glossary.

869. *Pour* [le] *porter.*

880. *de quelque maniere*=in some kind of manner. Verses 872-882 should be compared with the *Vita*: ». . . & omnes currebant obviam corpori sancto. Si quis autem infirmus illud sacratissimum corpus tangebat, protinus curabatur. Caeci visum recipiebant, daemonia ejiciebantur, & omnes infirmi, quacumque infirmitate detenti, tacto corpore sancto curabantur.« (169-173)

891-921. See note for verses 923-25, below.

920. For the order of these words (*en meïsmes la journee*), see Nyrop, V, # 414,1 rem. *Radaigaiz* was taken prisoner August 23, 406, and decapitated soon afterwards. See Walberg, p. 154 and the note for verses 923-25.

923-925. *The City of God (De Civitate Dei)*, Book V, Chapter 23, concerning the war in which Radagaisus, king of the Goths, a worshipper of demons, was conquered in one day, with all his mighty forces.
Cf.: "When Radagaisus, king of the Goths, having taken up his position very near to the city, with a vast and savage army, was already close upon the Romans, he was in one day so speedily and so thoroughly beaten, that, whilst not even one Roman was wounded, much less slain, far more than a hundred thousand of his army were prostrated, and he himself and his sons, having been captured [August 23, 406], were forthwith put to death [by decapitation], suffering the punishment they deserved . . ." See Marcus Dods, translator, *The City of God* (New York, 1948), p. 221.

928. *el*=*ceste victore* 922.

943-945. *Cassïen dit apertement* . . . Reference to the *De coenobiorum institutis*, tomus prior, liber IV (De Institutis renuntiantium, caput XXXVII), 197-98, and more specifically to the following passage of chapter 37 (Quod diabolus nostro fini semper insidietur, et nos ejus caput jugiter observare debeamus): »Versutus enim serpens (*Genes*. III) calcanea nostra semper observat, id est, insidiatur exitui nostro, et usque in finem vitae nostrae nos supplantare conatur. Et idcirco bene coepisse nihil proderit, nec pleno fervore renuntiationis arripuisse principia, si haec congruus etiam finis similiter non commendaverit atque concluserit . . .«.

962-964. Cf. Saint Matthieu, X, 22: »et vous serez haïs de tous, à cause de mon nom; mais celui-là sera sauvé qui persévérera jusqu'à la fin.«; and XXIV, 13: »Mais celui-là sera sauvé, qui persévérera jusqu'à la fin.«

967. Cf. Cassïen, op. cit., tomus prior, liber quartus (De Institutis Renuntiantium), caput XXXVI (Quod renuntiatio nostra nihil prosit, si eisdem quibus renuntiavimus implicemur), p. 197: »In hac quoque humilitate, ac patientia, qua ut suscipereris in monasterio decem diebus pro foribus perseverans multis lacrymis implorasti; non modo persistas, verum etiam proficias, atque succrescas. Satis enim miserum est ut cum debeas a rudimentis ac primordiis tuis provehi, et ad perfectionem tendere, etiam ab ipsis incipias ad inferiora recidere. Non enim qui coeperit haec, sed perseveraverit in his usque ad finem, hic salvus erit.« (Matth. X, and XXIV).

980-982. =carries him in one single day one half further than he had advanced in one year.

986. *la soue=sa perseverance* (v. 984); see Glossary.

990-992. *nos* is the indirect object of *pardonner* (991) as well as the direct object of *couronner* (992).

COMPLETE TABLE OF PROPER NAMES

Aglaes 104, mother of Saint Alexis. See Notes.

Aignel 325 (=l'Agneau de Dieu, Jésus-Christ), the Lamb of God, Christ.

Alexandre; le grant roi Alexandre 181, Alexander the Great.

Alexi 117, 391, 405 etc., Alexis (Saint).

Apocalipse 381, the Apocalypse or Revelation of Saint John the Divine (last book in the New Testament).

Archade 748, 800, 896, Arcadius, the Eastern Roman emperor, (395-408), son of Theodosius I the Great, and older brother of Honorius. See Honnouré, below.

Augustin 925, Saint Augustin, A.D. 354-430, one of the Latin fathers in the early Christian Church; author; bishop of Hippo in North Africa.

Boniface (Saint) 869, the Church of Saint Boniface in Rome.

Capitole (le) 646, the Capitoline (one of the 7 hills on which Rome was built).

Cassïen 943, 967, Latin writer (circa 360-435), author of the *Collationes*.

Cesar 182, Caius Julius Caesar (101-44 B.C.).

Chalemeine 182, Charles the Great (A.D. 742-814), king of the Franks 768-814; emperor of the Holy Roman Empire 800-814.

Chevalerie (Le Livre de Chevalerie) 94, 136, Book of Chivalry. See Notes.

Cilice 632, an ancient country in SE Asia Minor: later a Roman province.

Cité 924, Saint Augustin's *The City of God (De Civitate Dei)*. See Notes.

David 182, king of Israel (circa 1010-975? B.C.).

Dieu 33, 53, 64, etc., God.

Edisse 382, 447, 566, Edessa, city of Mesopotamia, in the province of Osrhoënne, now Rhoa or Orfa.

Esperit (Saint) 593, the Holy Spirit, the Holy Ghost.

Eufemïen 76, 191, 743, etc., father of Saint Alexis and husband of Aglaes, q.v.

Ewangile 962, Gospel.

Gotz 908; Goz 701, 917, Goths (one of the Teutonic people who, in the 3rd to the 5th centuries, invaded and settled in parts of the Roman Empire).

Grece 674, Greece.

Gregore 947, Gregory I, Saint ("Gregory the Great"), A.D. circa 540-604, Italian ecclesiastic: pope 590-604, author of the *Moralia in Hiob* and of the *Dialogue*.

Heliodore 508 (See Notes.)

Honnouré 748, Honorius (Flavius-Augustus), Roman emperor of the West (395-423). See Archade.

Innocent 746, Innocent I (Saint and Confessor), 42nd pope (402-417).

Inde 890, India.

Jeroeme 507, Saint Jerome, A.D. circa 340-420, church father, Christian ascetic and biblical scholar: chief preparer of the Vulgate version of the Bible.

Jhesu Crist 380, 740.

Jugement; au jour du Jugement 312, on the Day of Judgment.

Kirië eleïson 725, the brief petition "Lord, have mercy" used in various offices of the
   Greek Orthodox Church and of the Roman Catholic Church.
Laodice 377, 631, Laodicea, city of Syria, on the sea-coast (now Latikiah/Latakia or
   Ladikiveh/Ladikieh). See Notes (v. 633).
Mediëns 385 (=Mèdes), Medes (inhabitants of ancient Media).
Mort 838, personnification of death.
Pere; Saint Pere 717, The Church of Saint Peter in Rome.
Pol (saint) 1, Saint Paul; Saint Pol de Tharse 633: (the) Church of Saint Paul in Tarsus.
   See Tharse, below.
Prosper 7, Prosper of Aquitaine (Saint). See Notes.
Raagaiz 701; Radaigaiz 891, king of the Ostrogoths.
Rages 384, ancient name of the city of Edessa. See Edisse above, and Notes.
Rhin (le) 674, (the) Rhine.
Rommains (les) 185, 708, 912, etc., Romans (the).
Romme 75, 211, 405, etc., Rome.
Sapience (Le Livre de Sapience) 67, =Le Livre de la Sagesse, book of the Old Testament
   attributed to Salomon.
Sire 377, Syria.
Tharse 633,Tarsus, small city of Cilicia (ancient country and region on the coast of SE
   Asia Minor), on the historic Cydnus river. See Notes.
Theodose 784, Theodosius I ("the Great"), A.D. 346? -395, Roman emperor of the
   Eastern Roman Empire 379-395, father of Arcadius and Honorius.
Tusquenne 893, Tuscany (a region in West central Italy: formerly a great duchy).
Virge Marie 389, 588, (the) Blessed Virgin.
Ytaille 892; Ytale 704, Italy.

SELECTIVE GLOSSARY*

abatuz 876, past part. of *abatre*, throw or knock down.

abisme 380, destruction, ruin.

accroire 522, believe.

acerin 760 (lit.: d'acier), unshaken, resolute, constant.

achaison 622, 682, 858, occasion, time, reason (682).

[a]corde 366, accord.

acoustumance 585, habit.

adjutore 911, aid, help.

adoulee 424, past part. of *adouler* used as an adj., grief-stricken.

adresce 227, pres. 3 of adresser, direct.

advisoit; *s'advisoit de* 598: (=s'aviser de), think of. See Notes.

affiere 198, pres. subj. 3 of *afferir*, be suitable.

affolez 58, mad.

agaiz 702, ambushes, traps, ambuscades.

ajournee 736, dawn.

allegement 37, alleviation, relief.

allosee 383; allosez 169, past part. of *aloser* used as an adj., famous.

amen[u]isee 616, past part. of *amenuiser*, diminish.

ammonicion 777, admonition.

amortir 478, destroy, perish.

ançois 554, adverb, before.

anel 356, ring.

anuitement 571, nightfall.

apert; *en apert* 959, openly.

apertement 943, clearly.

apostole 746, 811, Pope.

apoursaër 236, variant form of OF *aporseoir*, possess.

appartenance 513, kinship, family relationship.

apprenge 163, present subj. 3 of *apprendre*.

arche 888, box, chest.

aromat 889, perfume.

assentement 119, agreement.

assigne 501, pres. ind. 3 of *assigner*, formulate, state precisely.

assise 904, past part., adj., fixed (set of time).

astelle 688, stick, piece of wood.

atant 601, thereupon, then.

aucun 615 (=quelque); adv.; *aucun poi* 615 (=quelque peu): somewhat (in some measure or degree, to some extent).

---

*Words appear in corrected manuscript form.

avisa 450, preterite 3 of *aviser*, recognize.

aviserent 448, pret. 6 of *aviser*.

avoia 122, preterite 3 of *avoier* (s'), se mettre à la voie, set out.

basme 890, balm (any aromatic or fragrant ointment).

beire 768; biere 828, 867, 879, coffin.

betez 28, past part. of *beter*, beat, harass, torment.

beut 668, preterite 3 of *boivre*, drink.

bois 197, hunting (in the forest or woods).

bons 266, what one desires, longs for.

boucle 358, buckle. See Notes.

bourg 953, town.

bru 558, daughter-in-law.

bruman 251, bridegroom (a newly married man). See Notes.

caroles 280, a kind of circular dance (ring-dance) with song.

celee 460, hiding (act of hiding), concealment.

celeement 373, secretly, quietly.

chaistives 854, s.f., unfortunate (one); chestive 839.

chaistiz 11, s.m., wretch.

chaitive 395, adj., miserable, worthy of pity, ragged.

chaloit 796, 875, imperfect ind. 3 of *chaleir*, matter, import, be of interest to.

change 654, imperative 2 of *changier*. See Notes.

chape 865, cloak.

charnelment 564, intimately (referring to parents and friends). Cf. OF *charnel* (de même
    sang, intime).

chartre 772, 779, 787, etc., charter, document. See Notes (v. 815).

chartre 816, prison.

chault 70, pres. ind. 3 of *chaleir/chaloir*. See *chaloit*, above.

cheüz 55, past part. of *chëoir*, fall.

chevalerousement 171, in knightly fashion, valiantly.

cimetire 600, churchyard (often used as a graveyard).

cogneu 859, perhaps *cognui*, preterite 1 of *conoistre*, know.

cognoisse 41, pres. subj. 3 of *conoistre*.

coite 573 (=couette), feather-bed.

coiz 21, quiet.

contretenir 813, resist, contest, refuse.

convertie 433, past part. of *convertir*, change.

corages 204, heart, mind, etc.; courage 493, thought; courage 289, intention, desire;
    avoir tres grant courage 289: have great desire.

corra 17, fut. 3 of *corre*, run.

cortines 284; courtines 573, curtain, tapestry, tapestried room.

coyement 281, quietly, secretly.

cremetouse 349, timid, timorous.

cremut 614, preterite 3 of *cremir/cremoir*, variant of *cremer*, fear.

cuida 632, preterite 3 of *cuidier*, expect, wish, have the intention of.

cuidoit 706, imperfect ind. of *cuidier*. See *cuida*, above.

cuisoient 683, imperfect ind. 6 of *cuire*, burn.

cure 254, 520, 805, desire, care; anxiety, solicitude (440); cures 484.

declaire 1, pres. ind. 3 of *declairier*, declare. See *desclaire*, below.

deduiz 217, rejoicings, merry-making.

deffermee 602, past part. of *deffremer/deffermer*, open.

delaisser 490, abandon.

138

delessance 989, s.f., abandonment, act of relinquishing.

delit 256, 369, 548, pleasure; deliz 987, pleasures.

delite 239, pres. 3 of *deliter*, delight, rejoice; *se delite en* 239: delight in.

delivree 277, past part. of *delivrer*, rid of.

demeinray 552, fut. 1 of *demener*, display.

demenee 459, past part. of *demener*. See *demeinray*, above.

dement 846, lamentation, grief, sorrow.

dementiers; *en dementiers que* 884: while (conj.).

demonstrance 741, designation, indication.

demoree 601, s.f., delay.

departie 861, s.f., departure.

departir 224, s.m., end, departure.

desclaire 957, 962, pres. 3 of *desclarier*, explain, clarify.

desconfire 90, 909, destroy, conquer.

desconfiture 154, discomfiture.

despisans 19, despicable, contemptible.

despisent 10, pres. ind. 6 of *despire*, despise.

despisimes 45, preterite 4 of *despire*. See *despisent*, above.

despit 953, past part. of *despire*.

desploïer 848, reveal.

desprise 395, deplorable, worthy of pity, ragged.

desserte 26, 313, 833, desert/deserts (reward or punishment deserved), fault.

destro[i]te 950, adj., harsh, rigorous.

desverie 48, madness.

devers; *par devers li* 287: near him, by his side.

devise 947, pres. 3 of *deviser*, relate, explain.

dient 468, pres. ind. 6 of *dire*, say.

dillacion 778, delay.

dire; *a l'istore dire* 378: according to history. See Notes.

discipline 686, punishment.

doctriner 353, instruct.

dolosoit (se) 550, imperfect 3 of *doloser*, lament for, grieve.

dont 170, adverb, therefore.

doubles; *a cent doubles* 656: in a hundredfold measure. See Notes.

doubte 708, 723, fear.

doubterent 906, preterite 6 of *doubter*, fear.

droitement 719, immediately, right away.

duiz 705, skilled, experienced.

eau[e] 683 (=eave/eve), water.

effors 707, strength, might (MF force).

embla (s') 280, 372, preterite 3 of *embler*, slip away. See Notes.

emboëz 620, past part. of *emboer*, soil (fig.), defile morally, as with sin; lit.: covered with mud.

emplouree 310 (=MF éplorée), adj., in tears, weeping, disconsolate.

emprise 805, past part. of *emprendre*, undertake, take.

encloistre 451, the enclosure of a church.

endemain (l') 606, s.m., next day (the).

enfers 880, s.m., (the) sick, cripple.

ennuit 428, tonight.

enquerre 796, inquire about, ask.

ensement 485, 558, 669, etc., adv., also, in the same way.

ensivon 343, imperative 4 of *ensivre*, follow.

ensuivre 245, 335, variant form of *ensivre*. See *ensivon*, above.

entendre; *entendre a* 125: give heed to, be intent upon.

entente 248, 493, desire.

enterin 659, complete, pure.

enteriner 354, accomplish completely.

entiedissant 769, pres. part. of OF *entiedir*, cool (Cf. MF attiédir).

entretant 821, 891, adv., meanwhile, during this time (written today entre temps).

entroubliast 672, imperfect subj. 3 of *entroblier*, forget.

envoiserie 552, pleasure, joy.

envoiseüre 223, beatitude, exalted happiness.

envoit 661, pres. subj. 3 of *envoier*, send.

es 147, 402, etc. (en les), art. contr., in the; es 393, 401 (=aux), to the.

esbatement 252, amusement, divertissement.

esbatoient 249, imperfect ind. 6 of *esbatre*, take one's pleasure.

escarboucle 357, s.m., carbuncle (the stone). See Notes.

eschiver 483, avoid.

esclargira 734, fut. 3 of *esclargir*, dawn, light up.

escoulourgeable 256, ephemeral, transitory.

escuëlle 687, bowl, bassin (for liquids).

eslite 594, adj., perfect, excellent.

eslut 340, preterite 3 of *eslir*, choose.

esmay 44, dismay.

esmurent (s') 908, preterite 6 of *esmovoir*, incite, be aroused.

esnué 644, naked (without adequate clothing), destitute.

esploitié 982, past part. of *esploitier*, accomplish, travel by sea.

espoëntez 35, past part. of *espoënter*, terrify.

espoventer 90, terrify.

essi 118, preterite 3 of *eissir/issir*, issue forth (be born).

estourmie 434, adj., agitated, perturbed.

estrace 540, trace.

estrange 568, 653, 791, adj., foreign, very different (568).

estroitement 670, severely, rigorously.

exemplaire 983, example.

exercitement 140, exercise, practice. See Notes.

exploite 949, pres. 3 of *exploitier*, enjoy (MF: jouir de).

faictement 545, adv., in this way, thus.

faiz 160 (=foiz).

farse; *faire la farse* (à) 634: trick, deceive.

fault 475, pres. ind. 3 of *faillir*, fail, lack.

fauvel 132, adj., hypocritical, false. See Notes.

feïst 207, imperfect subj. 3 of *faire*.

fenent 147, pres. ind. 6 of *fener*, cut, toss or ted (hay).

festoié 643, past part. of *festoier*, entertain sumptuously, feast.

feu 701 (=OF *fel*, nom. of *felon*), adj., cruel, pitiless, perfidious.

fiance 901, s.f., confidence.

forment 871, greatly, much.

fors 113, prep., except.

forvoient 468, pres. ind. 6 of *forvoiier*, go astray.

fournie 587, past part. of *fournir*, carry out, accomplish.

fournie 661, adj., perfect, complete.

frivoles 279, s.f., folly, levity.

garez 687 (=MF jarret), hams (of man), id est, the back of the thigh or the thigh and the buttock together.

gariz 881, past part. of *garir*, heal.

generaulté 710, generality.

genoillons; *a genoillons* 650: kneeling, on one's knees.

gesant 827, pres. part. of *gesir*, lie, lie down.

geü 793, past part. of *gesir*. See *gesant*, above.

gramoïement 510, grief, sorrow.

greignor 275, 334, 490, etc., adj. (comparative degree), greater.

greveuse 914, adj., grievous, serious.

grevoux 511, grievous, burdensome.

grief 703, s.m., sorrow, worry.

grief 896, adj., grievous, terrible.

haire 739, s.f., hair-shirt (a garment of coarse haircloth, worn next to the skin by ascetics and penitents).

hantent 348, pres. ind. 6 of *hanter*, dwell.

hé 822, exclamation.

hei 838, exclamation.

hers 115, s.m., heirs.

hostel 654, 666, s.m., dwelling (place of residence, home).

hosteler 652, lodge, provide hospitality.

illeques 633, 747, adv., there.

isnellement 782, adv., at once, promptly.

jut 884, preterite 3 of *gesir*.

laidenge 626, offense, wrong.

lange 792, woollen garment (esp. hair-shirt).

largement 243, adv., plentifully.

lassus 261, adv., there above.

leesce 228, joy, happiness.

legier; *de legier* 958: easily, quickly.

legieres; *legieres a* 353: easy to.

lermoïer 847, weep, shed tears.

lettreüre 142, literary knowledge, instruction, learning.

lettrez 146, adj., instructed (of persons).

leu 815, past part. of *lire*, read. See Notes.

libelle (d'injure) 623, libel (a formal written declaration or statement containing the allegation of a plaintiff or the grounds of a charge).

lié 294, pron., variant form of *lei*, à elle.

lieu 103, rank.

loënge 625, praise.

los 618, 622, praise, honour.

maille 918, half-penny.

maindre 310 (variant of *manoir*), dwell, stay.

mains 148; meins 148, (=moins).

mais; *mais que* + subj. 879 (=pourvu que): provided that.

maltraire 65, maltreatment.

malvestié 462, wickedness.

marguerite 333, pearl (fig.), gem (fig.).

marrie 542, 836, past part., adj., afflicted, grieved, sorrowful.

martire 896, slaughter, suffering.

matines 574, matins (the first of the seven canonical hours).

mehaing 942, wound, harm.

meinge 367, pres. subj. 3 of *manoir*, remain.

meïsmes; *en meïsmes la journee* 920: that very day. See Notes.

mendre 489 (=moindre).

mesaise 263, uncomfortable situation, discomfort, ill at ease.

meschief 326, 939, misfortune, harm.

mescogneü 856, unrecognized (one).

messages 441, messengers.

moleste 225, torment, harm.

mordable 255, adj., detrimental, scathing.

mort 921, killed.

mous 204 (=moeurs).

mouvant 690, pres. part. of *movoir*, cause, stir up.

mu 828, adj., speechless.

mué 22, past part. of *muer*, change.

nage 376, (sea-) voyage.

nage 970, 973, pres. 3 of *nagier*, navigate.

nagié 975, past part. of *nagier*. See *nage* (970), above.

neïs 203, adv., even.

nel 125, 435, 648, etc., contr. of *ne + le*.

neporquant 926, adv., none the less.

netes 352, adj., pure, unstained.

neuces 212, 221, 250, etc. (=noces), nuptial feast.

noise 690, quarrel, commotion.

nonne 110, 798, none, ninth (hour). See Notes.

nouveaulx 418, adj. (fem.). See Notes.

o 111, 164, 193, etc., prep., with.

occire 895, kill.

odit 575, preterite 3 of *oïr*, hear.

oïance; *en oïance* 742: in everyone's presence.

oiseuse 125, s.f., idleness.

oïst 206, imp. subj. 3 of oïr.

orant 603, pres. part. of *orer*, pray

orde 714 (fem. of OF *ort*), filthy, repugnant, horrible.

ordures 685, s.f., refuse, garbage.

orendroit 64, now, at present.

oroit 565, imp. ind. 3 of *orer*. See *orant*, above.

ostel 663, lodging.

ostelas (t') 830, preterite 2 of *osteler* (s'), lodge (oneself).

ou 398, 917, variant of *el* (=en le), in the.

oultreement 960, adv., entirely, absolutely.

oure 731, pres. 3 of *orer; en l'oure* 732: in an instant.

ourne; *a ourne* 973: steadily, regularly.

ouvré 844, past part. of *ovrer*, act.

parage 40, lineage.

pardurable 261, 592, eternal, everlasting; pardurables 15.

pardurablement 311, adv., eternally.

pareil 561, mate.

parfera 364, fut. 3 of *parfaire*, bring to completion, perfection.

parti 543, preterite 3 of *partir*, die.

partie 517, 764, 835, etc., side, direction; domain (517); *de l'autre partie* 835: in addition; *l'une partie* 939: one side.

partir 533, s.m., departure.

pencee 596 (=pensee).

penent 148, pres. ind. 6 of *pener* (gagner péniblement), earn, merit.

pener 444, pain oneself, exert oneself.

penous 368, painful.

pestel 688 (MF pilon), pestle.

peü 678, past part. of *paistre*, feed.

piece (grant) 114, a long time.

pis 204, adv., worse.

pitance 392, charity, alms, pity.

piteable 101, compassionate.

plenté 267, abundance; *a (grant) plenté* 219, 704: abundantly.

poair 184 (=poeir/pooir), power.

poi 131, 253, etc., adv. (=peu), little; *un poi* 263: a little; *qu'a poi que de deul ne parti* 543 (See Notes).

point 463, s.m., speck (very little bit or particle), iota.

porprise 387, past part. of *porprendre*, fortified, supplied, inhabited.

porsoians 167, possessors.

portal 567 (MF portail), s.m., portal (front gate or entrance of a church).

porveïst 671, imp. subj. 3 of *pourvoier*, q.v.

pose 967, pres. 3 of *poser*, affirm, state.

posnee 919, arrogance, bravado.

pourveance 237, providence.

pourvoier 757, provide, see to.

povair 893 (=povoir).

poverté 449, s.f., poverty, distress. See Notes.

premerain (le) 498, first (the); premeraine 296.

prestement 139, adv., quickly.

prise 590, pres. 3 of *priser*, esteem, value.

proces 773, 985, course; career, life (985).

prouvaille 341, proof.

quanque 842 (=quant que), relative pron., all that, whatsoever.

quel que; *de quel que maniere* 880; in some kind of manner.

quert 435, pres. ind. 3 of *querre*, seek.

quint 924, fifth. See Notes.

quoi; *pour quoi que* 658: provided that.

ramponez 31, raillery, jeer.

ravoie 190, pres. ind. 1 of *ravoier* (reflex.), return (to subject matter).

recroire 521, cease.

relief 655, leavings, scraps (from the table), leftovers.

remenant 399, remains from a meal, scraps.

repaire 561, 958; repeire 253, pres. ind. 3 of *repairier*, return; *repairier a dolour* 253: turn to grief.

repaissoient 106, imp. ind. 6 of *repaistre*, feed.

repeire 767, dwelling.

reprendre 421, find fault with, reprove.

requier 306, pres. ind. 1 of *requerre*, pray, implore.

requise 931, past part. of *requerre*, invoke, call upon.

resson 214, sound, noise.

retraire 151, 505, relate; withdraw from (505).

riviere 197, the hunting of waterfowl. Cf. *bois* 197, above.

roiaulx 32, adj., royal.

route 707, army.

rude 138, adj., brute (force).

saison 818, time.

santiesme 86, adj. (superlative degree), most holy, sacred.

sauf 963, adj., safe (spiritually).

sceüst 445, imp. subj. 3 of *savoir*.

segondement 729, adv., for the second time.

seg[r]etement 152, 959, adv., secretly, surreptitiously.

seins 82, s.m., insignia.

sentencie 93, pres. ind. 3 of *sentencier*, teach.

sepoulture 885, s.f., sepulcher (burial place).

septime 379, seventh. See Notes.

serie 453, 692, calm, gentle, soft.

sermonne 526, pres. ind. 1 of *sermoner*, speak, treat, discuss.

seult 444, pret. 3 of *savoir*.

si; *si que* 893: as far as (MF: jusqu'à).

sivra 324, fut. 3 of *sivre*, follow. See Notes.

soi 293, 427, 429, etc. (=sai), pres. ind. 1 of *savoir*, know.

soier 394, be seated.

somme 406, s.m., packsaddle.

soue (la) 986 (=la sienne), poss. pron., his. See Notes.

soustenement 557, support (MF soutien).

suaire 359, piece of cloth.

subtillesce 158, finesse, ingenuity.

souef 602, adv., gently, softly.

suer 330 (=soeur).

suffrage 937, support, assistance.

tabours 215 (=tambours), drums.

tant; *tant que* + subj. 360, 559, 579, 815: until; *tant que* 537: so that.

tempesté 242, tormented, anguished.

termes 534, times.

tesant 828, adj., silent (from *tacentem*, pres. part. of *tacere*, taire).

texi 986, preterite 3 of *tistre*, weave (fig.).

tienge 954, pres. subj. 3 of *tenir*.

tout; *tout* + subj. 206, 679, 801: although; *tout soit ce que* 518: even though; *sur touz* 483: especially.

traire 810, pull, take.

travail 722, travail (anguish, suffering).

trespassé 812, the dead man (id est, Saint Alexis).

trespassé 823, past part. of *trespasser*, die.

trespassement 775, death.

trespassera 732, fut. 3 of *trespasser*.

trieve 305 (=OF trive), respite, truce.

trompes 214, horns (musical).

truisse 765, pres. subj. 1 of *trover*, find.

turterelle 560, turtle-dove. See Notes.

uis 287, door.

us 192, custom.

144

user 390, pass (life).

valet 756, servant.

veïmes 46, preterite 4 of *veïr/voier*, q.v.

veïssent 580, imp. subj. 6 of *veïr/voier*, q.v.

verdour 479, s.f., verdure (flourishing condition; vigor).

vergondouse 350, adj., timid, easily embarrassed.

vez 45, 791, contraction of *veez*, voyez; *vez ci* 45, 791: here is, behold here.

ville 714, 954, adj., vile, base, despicable.

vi[l]té 610, shame, dishonour.

virge 319, 341, maiden, virgin.

voiables 16, adj., visible, apparent.

voie 231, s.m. (doloreux voie). See Notes.

voier 393, 758, see.

voir 438, 495, adj., true.

voire 926, adj., true.

voult 770, face.

vuider 286, empty.

BIBLIOGRAPHY*

Anglade, Joseph: Grammaire élémentaire de l'ancien français. Paris, 1965.
—, Grammaire de l'ancien provençal. Paris, 1921.
(Auctore Anonymo Conscripta). »Vita S. Alexii Confessoris,« Acta Sanctorum
    Bollandiorum, July, IV, 251-253.
Bloch, O. and W. v. Wartburg: Dictionnaire étymologique de la langue française. Paris,
    1964.
Bossu, Adam le: Le Jeu de la Feuillée, ed. by E. Langlois. Paris, 1966.
Curtius, E.R.: Zur Interpretation des Alexiusliedes, *ZRP*, LVI (1936), 113-137.
—, European Literature and the Latin Middle Ages, trans. by Willard R. Trask. New York
    and Evanston, 1962.
Desroches, l'Abbey: Extraits de plusieurs petits poèmes écrits à la fin du XIVe siècle par
    un prieur du Mont-Saint-Michel. Caen, 1839.
Dods, Marcus: The City of God. New York, 1948.
Faral, Ed.: Les Arts poétiques du XIIe et du XIIIe siècles. Paris, 1962.
—, Petite grammaire de l'ancien français. Paris, 1941.
Fouché, P.: Le verbe français. Etude morphologique. Paris, 1931.
Foulet, Lucien: Petite Syntaxe de l'ancien français. Paris, 1965.
Fremantle, W.H.: translator. A Select Library of Nicene and Post-Nicene Fathers of the
    Christian Church, v. VI. New York, 1912.
Godefroy, Frédéric: Lexique de l'ancien français. Paris, 1965.
Gossen, C.T.: Petite grammaire de l'ancien picard. Paris, 1951.
Hatcher, Anna Granville: The Old-French poem St. Alexis: A Mathematical Demonstration,
    Traditio, VIII (1952), 111-158.
Hauterive, Grandsaignes d': Dictionnaire d'ancien français. Paris, 1947.
Herz, J., ed.: De Saint Alexis, eine afrz. Alexiuslegende aus dem 13. Jrh. Frankfurt, 1879.
Jenkins, T.A.: La Chanson de Roland. Boston, 1924.
Koerting, G., rev. of J. Herz, ed.: De Saint Alexis, eine afrz. Alexiuslegende aus dem
    13. Jrh. Frankfurt, 1879, *ZRP*, IV (1880), 175-178.
Körting, G.: Lateinisch-Romanisches Wörterbuch. New York, 1923.
Langfors, Arthur, ed.: Le Roman de Fauvel. Paris, 1919. (Société des anciens textes
    français.)
Massmann, Hans Ferdinand: Sanct Alexiusleben in 8 gereimten mittelhochdeutschen
    Behandlungen. Quedlinburg und Leipzig, 1843.
Migne, J.P.: Patrologiae. t. XXII, XLIX, LI. Paris, 1945-1946.
Nyrop, Kr.: Grammaire historique de la langue française. 2 vols. Gyldendal, 1967.
Paris, G.: La Vie de St. Alexis, 7th ed., Paris, 1966.
—, La Vie de St. Alexis, Romania, VIII (1879), 163-180.
—, et L. Pannier. La vie de St. Alexis. Paris, 1872.

*Includes only works cited.

Pope, M.K.: From Latin to Modern French with especial consideration of Anglo-Norman. Manchester-England, 1952.

Robert, Ulysse, ed.: L'Art de Chevalerie. Paris, 1897. (Société des anciens textes français.)

Rösler, Margarete: Sankt Alexius. Halle/Saale, 1941.

Sacy, Lemaistre de, translator: La Sainte Bible. Paris, 1846.

Schwan-Behrens: Grammaire de l'ancien français. trad. O. Bloch, Leipzig, 1923.

Stebbins, Charles E.: The Oxford Version of the Vie de saint Alexis: An Old French Poem of the Thirteenth Century, Romania, 92 (1971), 1-36.

—, The Humanity of Saint Alexis in the Separation Scene of the 13th Century Old French Poem (Paris MS. 2162, Bibl. nat.) of the Vie de saint Alexis, Revue belge de Philologie et d'Histoire, XLIX (1971, No 3), 862-65.

Stimming, A.: Der anglonormannische Boeve de Hauntone. Halle, 1899.

Studer, P., ed.: Le Mystère d'Adam. Manchester-England, 1962.

Valentin, L.: Saint Prosper d'Aquitaine. Paris & Toulouse, 1900.

Walberg, E.: Contes pieux en vers du XIVe siècle, tirés du recueil intitulé le Tombel de Chartrose, Lund, 1946. (Acta Reg. Societatis Humaniorum litterarum. Lundensis, XLII, 77-105.)

—, Sur un mot français d'origine nordique, Studia Neophilologia, XVI (1943-44), 39-49.

APPENDIX

Vita S. Alexii Confessoris[1]
(Auctore Anonymo Conscripta)

1 Fuit Romae vir magnus, & nobilis Euphemianus nomine, dives valde, & primus in palatio Imperatoris. Erantque ei tria millia pueri, qui zonis cingebantur aureis, & sericis induebantur vestimentis. Hic namque erat justus & misericors, eleemosynas multas pauperibus erogans. Tres
5 per singulos dies mensae parabantur in domo ejus, orphanis, viduis, peregrinis & iter agentibus. Ipse vero ad horam nonam comedebat cum viris religiosis. Mulier autem ejus Aglaes nomine, religiosa, & timens Deum: & non erat illis filius, eo quod esset sterilis. Unde moerentes erant, & tristes, quod tantarum substantiarum, ac familiarum nullum haberent
10 heredem. Et ideo immensas cotidie largiebantur eleemosynas, orationibus quoque atque obsecrationibus insistentes Dominum deprecabantur, ut daret eis filium, qui succederet eis.

2 Quorum Deus secundum bonitatem suam, contritionem aspiciens, recordatus operum ipsorum, exaudivit eos, & concessit eis filium. Qui
15 nimis laetantes, gratias egerunt Deo, atque statuerunt, ut deinceps castum, & sanctum reliquum vitae suae tempus ducerent, ut Deus gauderet de illis, & de filio, quem dederat eis, & ut ultra ad invicem non accederent, sed in castitate perseverarent. Puer autem ut ad aetatem disciplinae congruam pervenit, tradiderunt eum ecclesiasticorum Sacra-
20 mentorum, ac liberalium disciplinarum magistris, & ita Deo largiente edoctus est, ut in omnibus philosophiae, & maxime spiritualibus floreret

---

1 I have included this Latin model (published in the *Acta Sanctorum Bollandiorum* ior July 17th, the feast day of Saint Alexis, pp. 251-253) to facilitate comparison with our texts. It has been printed in Massmann's *Sanct Alexiusleben in 8 gereimten mittelhochdeutschen Behandlungen.* (Quedlinburg und Leipzig, 1843), pp. 167-171. This book, however, is not readily available. Moreover, I found several typographical errors, e. g. *adspiciens* instead of aspiciens (p. 251); *discere* for *disserere, brandeo* for *prandeo, quosque* for *quousque* (=quo-usque) *iisdem* for *isdem* (p. 252); *coeci* instead of *caeci* (p. 253); etc. More serious is the omission of the following passage (p. 252,6): . . . "ut intrans, & exiens videret eum, praecipiens ut de mensa ejus pasceretur. Susceptus autem perseverabat in austeritate vitae suae . . ." The word "suae" which terminates the phrase immediately preceding this passage is the apparent cause of its omission.

studiis. Cum autem ad tempus adolescentiae accessisset, & eum nuptiali-
bus infulis aptum judicassent, elegerunt ei puellam ex genere imperiali,
& ornaverunt thalamum, & impositae sunt eis singulae coronae in templo
25 S. Bonifacii martyris per manus honoratissimorum sacerdotum, & sic
cum gaudio, & laetitia laetum duxerunt diem. Vespere autem facto dixit
Euphemianus filio suo: Intra, fili, in cubiculum, & visita sponsam tuam.
Ut autem intravit, coepit nobilissimus juvenis, & in Christo sapientissimus
instruere sponsam suam, & plura ei sacramenta disserere; deinde tradidit
30 ei annulum suum aureum, & rendam, id est caput baltei, quo cingebatur,
involuta in prandeo, & purpureo sudario, dixitque ei: Suscipe haec, &
conserva usque dum Domino placuerit: & Dominus sit inter nos.

    3 Post haec accepit de substantia sua, & discessit ad mare: accedens-
que ad mare, ascendensque navem, Deo prosperante pervenit Laodiciam,
35 & inde iter arripiens abiit[2] Edessam Syriae civitatem, ubi sine humano
opere imago Domini nostri Jesu Christi in sindone habebatur; quo perven-
iens, omnia, quae secum tulerat, pauperibus erogavit, & induens se
vestimenta vilissima, coepit sedere cum ceteris pauperibus ad atrium
sanctae Dei Genitricis Mariae. Sancta quoque Dei mysteria singulis diebus
40 Dominicis accipiebat, & de eleemosynis quae ei dabantur, quantum sibi
sufficeret, reservabat, cetera vero pauperibus erogabat. Post ejus dis-
cessionem facta est Romae inquisitio magna, & non invenientes eum,
misit pater ipsius pueros suos, ut per universas mundi partes inquirerent
eum. Quorum aliqui, dum venissent Edessam, viderunt eum inter ceteros
45 pauperes sedentem: & dantes [ei] eleemosynam, discesserunt, quia non
cognoverunt eum. Ipse autem home Dei cognoscens eos glorificabat
Deum, dicens: Gratias tibi ago Domine, qui me vocasti, & fecisti, ut
propter nomen tuum acciperem eleemosynam de servis meis; quaeso, ut
perficere digneris in me opus, quod coepisti. Reversi autem pueri nuncia-
50 verunt, non invenisse eum.

    4 Mater quoque ejus a die, qua discessit suus filius, sternens saccum
in pavimento cubiculi sui, sedensque super illud ejulans, & lamentans
dicebat: Vivit Dominus, quia ita manebo, donec cognoscam, quid actum
sit de filio meo. Sponsa vero ejus dixit ad socrum suam: Non egrediar
55 de domo tua, sed similabo me turturi, quae omnino alteri non copulatur,
dum ejus socius captus fuerit; sic & ego faciam, quousque sciam, quid
factum sit de dulcissimo conjuge meo. Ille namque home Dei in eodem,
quo dictum est atrio permansit in sancta conversatione, & vitae austeritate per decem & septem annos incognitus. [Postea vero volens Deus
60 revelare causam ipsius] imago, quae in honore sanctae Dei Genitricis
Mariae ibidem erat, paramonario ecclesiae dixit: Fac introire hominem
Dei, quia dignus est regno caelorum, & spiritus Dei requiescit super eum;

---

2 Undoubtedly a misprint for *adiit*.

nam & oratio ejus sicut incensum in conspectu Dei ascendit: exiensque
paramonarius, quaesivit eum, & non cognovit: & reversus intro, coepit
65 precari omnipotentis Dei clementiam, ut ostenderet eum illi. Iterum
ipsa imago ait: Ille qui sedet foris in ostio, ipse est.

5 Tunc paramonarius festinus egressus cognovit eum, & procidens ad
pedes ejus rogavit eum, ut in ecclesiam intraret; quod factum dum
cunctis innotesceret, & isdem homo Dei ab hominibus venerari coepisset,
70 humanam fugiens gloriam, occulte exiit de civitate Edessa, & venit
Laodiciam, ibique navem ascendens volebat in Tharsum Ciliciae ire, ut
in templo S. Pauli, quod ibidem est, maneret incognitus. Deo itaque
dispensante rapta est navis vento, & ducta est ad Romanum portum. Ut
autem ipse homo Dei se illuc venire perspexit, dixit in corde suo: Vivit
75 Dominus, quia alicui onerosus non ero, neque alibi ibo, nisi in domum
patris mei, quia cognitus illic non ero: & exiens venit, & obviavit patri
suo redeunti a palatio, circumdato obsequentium multitudine; & coepit
clamare, dicens: Serve Dei respice in me, & fac mecum misericordiam;
quia pauper sum, & peregrinus, & jube me suscipi in domo tua, ut Deus
80 benedicat annos tuos, & ei, quem habes in peregre, misereatur.

6 Pater vero ejus haec audiens, rememoratus est de filio suo, & com-
punctus jussit eum venire ad se, & ait pueris suis: Quis ex vobis curam
geret istius hominis? Vivit Dominus; quia liberum eum faciam, & de
domo mea accipiet hereditatem. Et deputato ei ministro, jussit eum
85 recipi, & facere ei grabatum in atrio domus suae, ut intrans, & exiens
videret eum, praecipiens ut de mensa ejus pasceretur. Susceptus autem
perseverabat in austeritate vitae suae, orationibus continuis, jejuniisque
& vigiliis indesessus. Pueri quoque coeperunt deridere eum, & aquam,
qua discos lavabant, super caput ejus fundebant, & multas injurias infere-
90 bant; quae omnia homo Dei propter amorem Domini libenter sustinebat;
sciebat enim quod antiquus humani generis inimicus has ei parabat
infidias: sicque fecit in domo patris sui incognitus alios decem, & septem
annos. Cum autem completum sibi tempus vitae suae cognovisset, postu-
lavit a deputato sibi ministro tomum chartae, & calamarem, & scripsit
95 per ordinem omnem vitam suam, qualiter respuerit nuptias, & qualiter
conversatus fuerit in peregrinatione, qualiterque contra voluntatem suam
redierit Romam, & in domo patris sui opprobria multa sustinuerit.

7 Quo peracto, volens Deus manifestare certamen, atque victoriam
ejus, Dominica die post Missarum solemnia completa, vox caelitus
100 insonuit in sanctuario dicens: Venite ad me omnes, qui laboratis, & onerati estis, & ego vos reficiam. Qua voce audita, nimio timore territi ceciderunt omnes in facies suas, clamantes: Kyrie eleison. Iterum secundo
vox facta est dicens: Quaerite hominem Dei, ut oret pro Roma; illucescente enim die parasceve Deo spiritum reddidit. Et tunc egressi qua-
105 esierunt eum, & non invenientes congregati sunt die parasceve omnes ad

ecclesiam, implorantes Dei clementiam, ut ostenderet eis, ubi esset
homo Dei. Tunc facta est vox ad eos dicens: In domo Euphemiani quaerite. Conversique ad Euphemianum dixerunt: In domo tua talem
gratiam habebas, & non ostendisti nobis. Ille quoque dicebat: Vivit
110 Dominus, nescio. Et statim vocavit priorem domus suae, & dixit ei: Scis
in domo mea aliquem, talem gratiam habentem. Ille autem se nescire
respondit. Tunc Imperatores Arcadius, & Honorius, qui eodem tempore
regebant Romanum imperium, una cum Pontifice Innocentio coeperunt
ire in domum Euphemiani, & diligenter exquirere de homine Dei.
115   8 Euphemianus autem praeivit cum pueris suis, ut sedes ordinaret,
& cum lampadibus, incenso quoque, & thuribulis obviam Imperatoribus,
& Pontifici exiret. Et cum illuc pervenissent, factum est silentium
magnum. Minister autem hominis Dei accessit ad dominum suum, dixitque ei: Vide, domine, ne forte sit ille, quem assignasti mihi; magna enim,
120 & laudabilia vidi eum operantem; per omnem enim Dominicam sancta
Dei munera accipiebat, jejuniisque semetipsum cruciabat; & injurias
multas atque molestias, a servis tuis illatas, libenter suscipiebat, atque
sustinebat. Ephemianus[3] autem haec audiens, festinus cucurrit ad eum;
& invenit eum jam defunctum, & accedens discooperuit faciem ejus,
125 & vidit vultum ipsius velut lampadem lucentem, vel sicut vultum angeli
Dei: habebatque in manu brevem scripturam, & voluit eam ab eo accipere,
& non valuit. Quo stupefactus, atque timore percussus, cito reversus ad
Imperatores dixit: Quem quaerebamus, invenimus; & narravit eis quae ei
recitata fuerant de eo a ministro, & qualiter defunctum eum invenisset,
130 tomumque in manu habentem, & eum nequivisset ab eo accipere.
   9 Tunc Imperatores, & Pontifex cum Euphemiano perrexerunt ad
locum, ubi jacebat, steteruntque ante grabatum, & dixerunt: Quamvis
peccatores simus, gubernacula tamen regni gerimus; iste autem Pontifex,
pater universalis est; da nobis chartam, ut sciamus quae in ea scripta sunt.
135 Et accedens Pontifex, accepit chartam de manu ejus, & dedit chartulario
sanctae Romanae Ecclesiae, nomine Ethio, ut legeret eam; & facto
silentio magno lecta est coram omnibus. Euphemianus autem pater ejus,
ut audivit verba chartae, factus exanimis cecidit in terram, & surgens
scidit vestimenta sua, coepitque canos capitis sui evellere, barbam tra-
140 here, atque semetipsum discerpere: & corruens super ipsum corpus
clamabat: Heu me Domine [Deus] meus, quare mihi sic fecisti, & quare
ita contristasti animam meam, & per tot annos suspiria, & gemitus incussisti mihi? Ego enim sperabam aliquando audire vocem tuam, & de te
agnitum habere, ubicumque esses, & nunc video te custodem senecturis
145 meae in grabato jacentem, & mihi non loquentem. Heu me! qualem
consolationem in corde meo ponam?

---

3 Misprint for *Euphemianus.*

152

10 Mater vero ejus haec audiens, quasi leaena rumpens rete, ita
scissis vestibus exiens, coma dissoluta ad caelum oculos levabat, & cum
prae nimia multitudine ad sanctum corpus adire non posset, clamabat:
150 Date mihi viri Dei aditum, ut videam consolationem animae meae, ut
videam filium meum, qui suxit ubera mea. Et cum pervenisset ad corpus,
incumbens super illud, clamabat: Heu me! fili, lumen oculorum meorum,
quare sic nobis fecisti? Videbas patrem tuum, & me miserabiliter lach-
rymantes. & non ostendebas teipsum nobis; servi tui te injuriabant,
155 & sustinebas. Et iterum atque iterum prosternebat se super corpus, &
nunc brachia super illud expandebat, nunc manibus vultum angelicum
contrectabat, osculansque clamabat: Plorate mecum omnes, qui adestis;
quia decem & septem annos eum in domo mea habui, & non cognovi,
quod unicus filius meus esset, sed servi ejus injuriabant, alapis percutie-
160 bant eum, & sputa in faciem ejus jactabant. Heu me! Quis dabit oculis
meis fontem lachrymarum? ut plangam die, ac nocte dolorem animae
meae. Sponsa quoque ejus induta veste Adriatica, cucurrit plorans, &
dicens: Heu me! quia hodie desolata sum, & apparui vidua. Jam non
habeo in quem aspiciam, nec in quem oculos levem. Nunc ruptum est
165 speculum meum, & periit spes mea; amodo coepit dolor, qui finem non
habet. Populus autem videns haec, lachrymabiliter flebat.
11 Tunc Pontifex cum Imperatoribus posuerunt corpus in ornato
feretro, & duxerunt in mediam civitatem, & nunciatum est populo,
inventum esse hominem Dei, quem civitas tota quaerebat, & omnes curre-
170 bant obviam corpori sancto. Si quis autem infirmus illud sacratissimum
corpus tangebat, protinus curabatur. Caeci visum recipiebant, daemonia
ejiciebantur, & omnes infirmi, quacumque infirmitate detenti, tacto
corpore sancto curabantur. Imperatores autem tanta mirabilia videntes,
coeperunt per se cum Pontifice, lectum portare, quatenus & ipsi sancti-
175 ficarentur ab eodem corpore sancto. Et jusserunt copiam auri, argentique
in plateis spargere, ut turbae occuparentur amore pecuniae, & sinerent
eum perduci ad ecclesiam; sed plebs amore pecuniae seposito, magis ac
magis ad tactum sanctissimi corporis irruebant: & sic cum magno
labore ad templum sancti Bonifacii martyris perduxerunt, & illic per
180 septem dies in Dei laudibus persistentes operati sunt monumentum de
auro, & gemmis pretiosis, in quo sacratissimum illud corpus cum magna
veneratione collocaverunt die xiv mensis Julii. De ipso quoque monu-
mento ita suavissimus odor fragravit, acsi esset omnibus aromatibus
plenum. Tunc populi jucundantes, maximas Domino gratias agebant, qui
185 tale populo suo conferre dignatus est subsidium, per quod omnis quicum-
que sincera mentis intentione deprecatus fuerit, petitionis effectum
sine dubio consequatur. Per Dominum nostrum.